HOME GROWN GARDENING

ATTRACTING BIRDS AND BUTTERFLIES

HOME GROWN GARDENING

ATTRACTING BIRDS AND BUTTERFLIES

HOW TO PLANT A BACKYARD HABITAT TO ATTRACT WINGED WILDLIFE

BARBARA ELLIS

Houghton Mifflin Harcourt

BOSTON NEW YORK 2019

For information about permission to reproduce selections from this book, write to
trade.permissions@hmhco.com or to Permissions, Houghton Mifflin Harcourt
Publishing Company, 3 Park Avenue, 19th Floor, New York, New York 10016.

www.hmhbooks.com

Library of Congress Cataloging-in-Publication Data
Names: Ellis, Barbara W., author.
Title: Attracting birds and butterflies / Barbara Ellis.
Description: [Revised edition] | Boston ; New York :
Houghton MifflinHarcourt, 2019. | Series: Home grown gardening | Includes index.
Identifiers: LCCN 2019009429 (print) | LCCN 2019015386 (ebook) |
ISBN 9780358101888 (ebook) | ISBN 9780358106425 (trade paper)
Subjects: LCSH: Gardening to attract birds. | Butterfly gardening.
Classification: LCC QL676.5 (ebook) | LCC QL676.5 .E57 2019 (print) |
DDC 595.78/9—dc23
LC record available at https://lccn.loc.gov/2019009429

ISBN 978-0-358-10642-5

Printed in China

SCP 10 9 8 7 6 5 4 3 2 1

CONTENTS

INTRODUCTION

To songbirds, hummingbirds, butterflies, and other wildlife, the typical suburban landscape resembles an unfriendly desert. Close-cropped lawns, sheared foundation shrubs, and deadheaded flowers mean no place to nest, no food to eat, and nowhere to hide. Fortunately, any landscape can become a haven for winged wildlife—and for the people who share it. Wildlife-friendly yards and gardens are filled with flowers from spring to frost, brilliant berries, and glistening water—along with dazzling birds and butterflies. Since lower maintenance is another advantage, it's easy to see how both wildlife and people benefit from such a space. Use this book as a guide to help you plant a landscape that welcomes winged wildlife. In the process, you'll create a garden that enriches your own life as well.

The seeds of *Rudbeckia nitida* 'Herbstsonne' ('Autumn Sun' coneflower) attract goldfinches.

WELCOMING WINGED WILDLIFE

chapter one

reating a garden that welcomes songbirds, hummingbirds, and butterflies may seem like a confusing and complicated task, but the principles involved are relatively simple. In essence, birds and butterflies need the same basic things you do to feel at home in a new place—they just define them a little differently.

FIRST AND FOREMOST, they need a ready supply of food. While you expect a well-stocked refrigerator and pantry, birds and butterflies look to the flowers, foliage, berries, and seeds in your garden for their food.

They also need fresh water for drinking and bathing. To really settle in and make your garden home, they also need cover in the form of trees and shrubs to feel safe and secure, as well as places to raise their families.

In this chapter, you'll learn more about the basic needs of songbirds, hummingbirds, and butterflies. Of course, you can't confine any of these fascinating creatures to your backyard, but you can use these principles to create a yard that will attract them and make them feel at home. In chapters 2, 3, and 4, you'll find specific recommendations for attracting birds, hummingbirds, and butterflies, including lists of the plants they prefer.

To attract hummingbirds, like this ruby-throat, plant a variety of annuals and perennials, such as *Agastache* 'Kudos Coral', or hyssop, also known as hummingbird mint.

food

IF BIRDS AND BUTTERFLIES occasionally pass through your yard but never seem to stay, it may be because you have been offering them only overnight accommodations—a passing meal, perhaps—instead of a varied, long-term food supply. To start designing plantings that attract birds and butterflies, it helps to know what they like to see on the menu. Flowers, fruits, seeds, and nuts from plantings of annuals, perennials, trees, shrubs, and vines—as well as weeds and grasses—are a good place to start. Garden insects and soil-dwellers such as earthworms, wireworms, beetles, and other organisms are also important menu items.

TIPS FOR SUCCESS

Weeds aren't normally welcomed in gardens, but many weeds attract birds and butterflies in abundance because of their seeds, their nectar, or the insects they attract. Set aside space for field species such as Queen Anne's lace, black-eyed Susans, native asters, goldenrods, milkweeds, and yarrows. Yellow-flowered *Impatiens pallida* and orange-flowered *I. capensis*, both commonly called jewelweed, are good plants for attracting hummingbirds. Both grow in moist to wet soil in shade.

Jewelweed (*Impatiens capensis*).

This informal planting offers food to birds and butterflies. Coneflowers (*Echinacea purpurea* and *Rudbeckia fulgida*) provide seeds for birds and nectar for butterflies. Butterflies visit the catmint (*Nepeta* spp.) and sedum (*Sedum* spp.).

Hummingbirds and butterflies, of course, depend on flowers for nectar, but hummingbirds also eat a large number of insects, including weevils, gnats, aphids, and mosquitoes. In addition to flowers for nectar, adult butterflies need plants that will feed their larvae.

Mexican bush sage (*Salvia leucantha*) is a favorite of hummingbirds and butterflies because of its arcing spikes borne from late summer until first frost.

The leaves of Queen Anne's lace (*Daucus carota*) are an important food for hungry swallowtail butterfly larvae. Consider growing it in a meadowlike planting, which will also attract a variety of seed-eating birds such as sparrows and juncos.

To encourage birds to stick around, you need to create a landscape that will allow them to find food daily. Birds that overwinter in your garden need to find food 365 days of the year. In fact, small birds such as chickadees and nuthatches eat almost constantly during daylight hours,

New England asters (*Aster novae-angliae*) provide a ready source of late summer to fall nectar for a variety of butterflies such as this variegated fritillary. After the flowers fade, songbirds can feast on the seeds well into winter.

Common winterberry (*Ilex verticillata*) provides a bounty of winter berries for hungry birds and adds plenty of eye-catching color to the landscape in the process.

especially in the winter. Winter bird feeding is just part of the picture for overwintering species. Variety is also important. Many birds eat berries and other fruits that persist on trees and shrubs through winter. Woodpeckers and many songbirds scour tree trunks and branches for insect eggs and overwintering larvae.

Migratory songbirds need food for varying amounts of time: Warblers may pass through your yard and feast on insects for only a few weeks in spring and fall. Songbirds that come to your region to build nests and raise families need food to feed their hungry broods for several months. Hummingbirds and butterflies need flowers for nectar from spring to fall in some areas.

Flowering dogwoods (*Cornus florida)* produce berries in late summer and fall that attract more than ninety species of birds, including catbirds, mockingbirds, robins, thrushes, woodpeckers, bluebirds, and cardinals.

PLANNING FOOD SOURCES

To create a landscape that provides birds and other wildlife with a guaranteed, year-round food supply, you need to plant an assortment of species that provide seeds, berries, nuts, or other food throughout the year. Planting a diverse selection helps ensure that a variety of food sources is always available. Feeding birds seeds and suet—in winter or all year—not only supplements what they find in your yard, but also makes it easy for you to enjoy watching them from indoors.

The best way to start planning a food supply for your guests is to take an inventory of what is already growing in your yard. Draw a rough map of your property in a loose-leaf notebook. Take it outdoors and make notes about what plants are growing in your yard. (Use a field guide or garden book to identify plants you're not familiar with.) Also note what types of habitat you have available. Is your yard a mix of sun and shade, all sunny, or all shady?

Then use the lists in this book to determine which plants in your yard already provide food for birds and butterflies, and which do not. For example, 'Kwanzan' cherries are popular ornamental trees that bear large rounded clusters of double pink flowers in spring. But the flowers are sterile and do not yield berries for birds. Chokecherries (*Prunus virginiana*) and pin cherries (*P. pensylvanica*) not only have white spring flowers, but also produce berries relished by many birds, including bluebirds, mockingbirds, and catbirds. You may want to remove some plants that do not provide food in order to make room for some that do.

Also note the season or seasons that the food is available. Making a chart or checklist in your notebook is a good way to do this. It's a good idea to assign different pages to different seasons, starting each page with the food-producing plants already growing in your yard. Then list plants you can add. Concentrate first on adding plants that provide food during seasons when nothing much is available in your yard. For example, if you have plenty of midsummer nectar sources for hummingbirds but nothing in early summer or fall, you may want to plant columbines (*Aquilegia* spp.) and foxgloves (*Digitalis* spp.) for spring and early summer and annual salvias for fall. If butterfly larvae plants are in short supply, you might plant extra parsley and dill to feed the larvae of swallowtail butterflies. You will find a list of plants for butterfly larvae in chapter 4.

Keep your map and notes handy. That way you can keep records about plants to add to your landscape in one place. You may also want to add sections for jotting down notes about birds or other wildlife you see. Include some pockets so you can tuck in notes and clippings that provide ideas for improving your wildlife habitat.

PROVIDING SAFE FOOD

Organic gardening is another essential ingredient in any landscape that welcomes birds and butterflies. One reason is that organic gardens are teeming with insects and other organisms that birds enjoy. Since organic gardeners avoid chemical pesticides, fungicides, and fertilizers, birds are guaranteed a safe, chemical-free food supply, and butterfly populations aren't affected.

Many annuals attract both hummingbirds and butterflies. This garden includes easy-to-grow cosmos (*Cosmos bipinnatus*).

Although any system that encourages insects may sound like a surefire recipe for disaster, birds will help control garden pests, along with annoying insects like gnats and mosquitoes. Many of the insects that thrive in an organic garden are beneficial; that is, they eat or parasitize pest insects and help keep populations in check. Other beneficial insects—honeybees most notably—pollinate flowers, which creates seeds and berries for birds to eat.

Good gardening practices are the cornerstones of organic gardening. Instead of waging war against pests and diseases with an arsenal of chemicals, organic gardeners seek to nudge the ecosystem into a healthy balance rather than bludgeon it into submission. Preventive techniques like building healthy soil are important first lines of defense against pests. (Healthy soil that is rich in organic matter is also rich in earthworms and other soil-dwellers, important sources of food for birds.) Beneficial insects and animals are welcomed as allies. "Soft" controls, such as soaps, oils, and beneficial organisms such as parasitic nematodes, are used before stronger, plant-derived sprays and dusts, such as rotenone and sabadilla. Bt (*Bacillus thuringiensis*) is a toxin-producing pesticide that is generally considered safe, but keep in mind that Bt kills butterfly larvae along with larvae of pest insects such as cabbage loopers. Avoid its use entirely, or use it only in very controlled applications in the vegetable garden. Avoid even organically acceptable plant-derived sprays for the same reason.

water

TO MOST WILDLIFE, the average suburban landscape looks like a desert. A yard covered in lawn grass with a few foundation shrubs simply doesn't provide many opportunities for bathing and drinking. Birds drink and bathe in the shallow water of ponds, streams, ditches, and puddles, as well as in birdbaths and garden pools. They'll even drink water that collects on the cupped foliage of plants like hostas after a rainstorm. Many species, including warblers, also "leaf bathe" by fluttering among the wet leaves of trees and shrubs after a rainstorm. In desert areas, birds depend on the leaves of succulent plants and the moisture contained in insects for their water needs. Many small desert species also leaf bathe.

Butterflies need water too. Nectar and water found on flower petals provide much of what they drink. You'll also see them gathered on sandbars along a stream, on the muddy bank of a pond, or around a puddle of water, engaged in an activity called puddling, in which they drink water and take up mineral salts.

Fortunately, it's easy to add water sources to your garden. A birdbath is a good place to start. Most birds prefer a spot in a clearing, so position it in a sunny spot about 15 feet from trees and shrubs. That way, bathing birds can keep an eye out for

A ready supply of clean water is an essential ingredient in any landscape that is designed to attract birds, butterflies, and other wildlife.

PROVIDING WATER IN WINTER

Providing water for birds in winter is relatively easy now that safe, economical birdbath heaters are readily available at wild bird centers, hardware stores, and garden centers. These heaters generally feature thermostats that keep water from freezing even in subzero temperatures while still conserving energy. Select a model that shuts off automatically when it runs out of water, and connect heaters only to properly grounded outlets. Be sure to clean the birdbath throughout the winter to provide safe water for drinking and bathing.

predators and will have time to fly for cover. (Birds can't fly quickly with wet feathers.) Other species, including thrushes, prefer a ground-level spot under cover of dense shrubbery, so they can drop down and bathe unnoticed.

A natural depression in the ground that stays moist is natural look-ing and a good alternative for a conventional birdbath. You can keep a moist spot filled with a garden hose even in dry weather. If you don't have an area that stays moist naturally, create one by digging out a shal-low area, lining it with concrete, and keeping it filled with clean water.

Keep in mind that birds are wary of water that is more than 2 or 3 inches deep. Add a few good-sized stones that emerge from the water for smaller birds, butterflies, and beneficial insects to land on. Many species will also alight on a twig attached to the edge of a birdbath before entering the water to bathe. Whether you select a conventional birdbath or a ground-level pool, be sure it has rough edges so birds can walk up to the water without slipping.

It is important to remember that birds need *clean* water. For this reason, locate your birdbath within reach of a hose so it is easy to keep filled and clean.

Empty and scrub out birdbaths every 2 to 3 days, especially in the summer, to prevent bacteria and algae from fouling the water. Never use cleaning chemicals to wash a birdbath, as they may endanger the very birds you are trying to attract.

MAKING WATER MORE ATTRACTIVE

Incorporating the sound and sight of moving water will increase the number of birds attracted to your water feature. Even a leaky bucket hung over a birdbath will increase its "bird appeal." Simply hang up a bucket or jug with a pin-sized hole and keep it filled with water. The sound of slowly dripping water will attract birds. A dripping hose can be used the same way.

Many wild bird centers, hardware stores, and nurseries sell a variety of small, recirculating fountains and sprayers that can be used in a birdbath or a small pond. Hummingbirds are particularly attracted to sprayers and will bathe by simply flying through the spray without landing at all.

For the serious bird gardener, a backyard pond or water garden is a possibility. Surrounded by natural-looking plantings and filled with water lilies and fish, it can be the perfect centerpiece for a bird garden. Be sure to design a shallow "beach" or other area for birds to bathe in with water that is no more than 3 inches deep. (Birds generally cannot reach the water in conventional water gardens, which have steep sides.) A fountain or small waterfall is easy to incorporate and will attract birds with the sound of moving water.

cover and nest sites

BOTH BIRDS AND BUTTERFLIES NEED COVER, or shelter, for protection from the elements as well as to escape predators. Birds also need secure places to roost at night and raise their young. Here again, the average suburban yard is a wasteland; a tree in the front yard surrounded by lawn may provide room for a single nest, but not much more.

Mixed plantings of trees, shrubs, vines, perennials, annuals, and grasses provide ideal cover and many options for nest sites for a wide variety of birds. The best plants to choose also provide food—seeds, nuts, berries, nectar. Plants with densely branching or suckering habits

Dense plantings of trees and shrubs—both deciduous and evergreen—provide nest sites and protection from winter winds.

Evergreens such as American holly *(Ilex opaca)* that provide wind protection, safe nest sites, and winter berries are especially valuable wildlife plants.

are excellent because they produce thick cover. For nest sites, thorns are a plus, because they provide extra predator protection. For this reason, shrub roses and hawthorns (*Crataegus* spp.) are excellent choices.

Needle- and broad-leaved evergreen trees and shrubs, such as white pines, arborvitae, spruce, junipers, cedars, and hollies, provide essential winter protection as well as food. (Birds eat the seeds, berries, and sap of many of these plants.) Different species of birds need different types of cover, however. Species like meadowlarks, field sparrows, and bobolinks prefer grassy meadow or prairie habitat for feeding and nesting.

arranging cover plants

THE WAY YOU ARRANGE THE PLANTS IN YOUR YARD will have an effect on how appealing it is to birds, butterflies, and other wildlife. Once again, variety is the key to success—both in the number of different plants you select and in the types of habitats you create.

To determine what the best arrangement is for your yard, turn to the rough map you made. Draw arrows to indicate the prevailing winter winds in your area—winds from the northwest are common throughout the country; areas along the East Coast may have winds that come from the east, off the Atlantic, that are most troublesome in winter. Ideally, plantings should provide protection from prevailing winds, especially in the winter. Butterflies also benefit from wind protection in summer, so they aren't buffeted about by breezes.

Rows of evergreens or mixed plantings of evergreens and tall deciduous trees are very effective for blocking wind. If the prevailing winter winds in your region come from the northwest, plant them along the north and west sides of your yard. A row of evergreens will work, but a mixed planting in a free-form shape is more natural looking. A fifty-fifty mix of deciduous and evergreen species is ideal.

To create a really effective barrier that is also rich in food and nest sites, mix in smaller trees and shrubs in layers along the front (leeward) side. Small-fruited crab apples, shrub roses, serviceberries (*Amelanchier* spp.), and deciduous hollies are all ideal for planting along a windbreak. Add beds of perennials and annuals in front that provide seeds and nectar. Or plant a large sunny area with meadow or prairie plants.

Every yard presents opportunities for creating different types of habitats that welcome winged wildlife. The more kinds of plantings you have, the more varied wildlife your yard will attract. You can underplant trees with shade-loving plants, fill a wet area with bog plants, and plant a sunny garden designed to attract hummingbirds, butterflies, and seed-eating birds. Look at the conditions that prevail in your yard and your region for ideas. Nature centers, botanical gardens, and wild bird centers have books and other information about plants and plant communities that are native to your region. Here are some ideas to consider.

SHADE PLANTINGS

Underplanting a wooded lot with food-rich species is an ideal way to create a bird-friendly landscape. Woodland edges are especially rich habitats for both birds and butterflies, because they feature both sun

Shady areas can be made attractive to many songbirds by adding shrubs as well as perennials such as hostas and cranesbill (*Geranium*).

TIPS FOR SUCCESS

Many birds depend on leaf litter, especially in wooded areas, so don't routinely rake it out of beds, borders, shade gardens, or wooded areas. Decomposing leaves return essential organic matter to the soil, but for birds leaf litter also contains an abundance of food. Birds such as thrushes, towhees, and fox sparrows hunt through it to find insects, fallen seeds, and berries to eat. The larvae of many insects overwinter in leaf litter—including some butterfly species: raking it up not only eliminates a winter food source, but also diminishes summer populations.

and shade plants and offer plenty of cover. Adding berried shrubs to an existing shade garden is another option. Even a yard that has only a few shade trees underplanted with lawn can be made more hospitable for birds. (Cutting down on lawn maintenance is an added benefit!) Remove the grass under one or more trees. Then underplant with a mix of shade-tolerant shrubs and small trees to create shady islands of plants. Add shade-loving perennials, ground covers, wildflowers, and annuals.

Shrubs and trees recommended for shady sites include dogwoods, azaleas and rhododendrons, shade-tolerant viburnums, hollies (*Ilex* spp.), blueberries (*Vaccinium* spp.), Oregon grape holly (*Mahonia aquifolium*), and spicebush (*Lindera benzoin*). Crab apples (*Malus* spp.) and hawthorns (*Crataegus* spp.) can be planted in clearings and along woodland edges. Perennials include hostas, violets, columbines, and wild strawberries (*Fragaria virginiana*). Northern sea oats (*Chasmanthium latifolium*) is a shade-tolerant ornamental grass.

SUN PLANTINGS

A bounty of sun-loving plants will attract songbirds, hummingbirds, and butterflies, and these plants can be incorporated into a landscape in many ways. Flower beds and borders are an obvious choice for sunny

Meadow plantings attract plenty of wildlife, including seed-eating birds, and butterflies seeking nectar and host plants for their larvae. Birds such as field sparrows will nest among the tall grasses and wildflowers.

sites. Plant them around a patio or birdbath, along a windbreak planting of trees and shrubs, or all along the back boundary of your yard. To add variety and all-season interest, try mixing in small trees and shrubs.

For a more natural look, consider meadow or prairie-like plantings. The best way to turn a small patch of lawn into meadow or prairie is to start with flower transplants, either homegrown or store-bought. For larger areas, seed is the only economical way to go.

Select a mix of wildflowers and native grasses that has been developed for your region of the country. Avoid generic mixes developed for the entire country or "instant" meadow mixes, which generally contain mostly annuals. (See "Flowers, Grasses, and Vines for a Bird Garden" on page 80 for a list of species to consider planting.)

To plant transplants or sow seeds, start by preparing the soil in midsummer. First mark out the area you plan to plant, mow it as close as possible, then till it under. Then either wait two weeks, till shallowly again to kill newly sprouted weeds, and repeat the tilling process two or three more times to control weeds; or lay four layers of newspaper on the ground and spread about an inch of mature compost on top.

Plant transplants in fall or early spring—whenever you commonly plant perennials. Use a bulb planter or a trowel to dig holes for the plants. Arrange the plants in a random pattern, clumping groups of the same plants together in some areas. Water and then mulch the plants with organic mulch—up to but not touching the stems—to control weeds.

To seed a meadow, in Zone 3 and south, plan to have the soil ready to sow one month before the first frost of fall. Or prepare the soil in midsummer and sow in early spring the following year, as soon as you can work the soil. Top-dress with a quarter-inch layer of topsoil or finely screened compost, and water it well.

Cut your new meadow annually in winter or very early spring; you may need to use a string trimmer first, if it's quite high, then mow.

Salvia and dahlias are ideal plants for attracting hummingbirds.

growing with your design

TRYING TO TRANSFORM A BARREN LANDSCAPE into a haven for birds and butterflies overnight is an easy way to become frustrated. Instead of trying to replant everything at once, plan on making gradual changes over the course of several planting seasons. Use the notes you have made about food plants you have, and ones you want to plant, as a guide. You may also want to consult a book on garden design and draw up a master plan to follow over the years.

Identify one or two areas to concentrate on for the first year. If you already have a barrier of evergreens along the northwest side of your property, for example, you might want to spend your time and energy adding trees and shrubs in front of it that will provide additional cover and food. If you have a single tree in the front yard, you could consider adding more trees and underplanting with berry-producing shrubs and ground covers.

Plan to add plants gradually as your budget and time allow. Buy the largest plants you can afford, and only as many as you can care for at one time. Proper soil preparation, watering, mulching, and weeding are all essential to getting plants off to a good start. You'll be rewarded with much larger, healthier plants if you lavish care on a few specimens at a time instead of providing the bare minimum for a host of plants. For large, expensive trees, you may consider having a nursery do the planting. Not only do they handle the sweat and strain of planting, they also have equipment to handle larger specimens with the least amount of stress on the plant. Most nurseries offer a replacement guarantee for trees and shrubs they plant; some guarantee even those they don't plant.

Over time, you'll find that growing a garden that welcomes winged wildlife provides benefits for people as well as birds. The plants that attract songbirds, hummingbirds, and butterflies have a rich natural beauty, and a garden designed to be full of flowers and fruits—as well as flashing feathers and glittering wings—has unmatched appeal. Natural

Bleeding heart (*Dicentra eximia*) blooms in spring and summer and will attract butterflies and hummingbirds.

insect control, low maintenance, increased property value, and energy conservation from wind-break plantings are other benefits of a well-planned wildlife garden.

Fine-tuning your bird garden can become a lifelong pursuit, and watching the birds that visit can become an entertaining hobby. You may want to keep notes on the birds you see, behaviors you observe, and the plants they visit most often. Over the years, you will undoubtedly find new trees, shrubs, vines, perennials, and annuals to add, or new combinations of plants to try, that will improve the habitats you've created. Trees and shrubs will grow larger, bear more fruit, and provide opportunities for underplanting with shade-tolerant species. Enjoy your changing land-scape and the wildlife that it attracts.

CREATING A
BIRD GARDEN

chapter two

Planting trees, shrubs, vines, and flowers that appeal to birds is the most important step you can take toward creating a backyard bird haven. Adding a source of fresh, clean water is a second essential step. Chapter 1 covered the basics of how to design a bird garden and arrange the plants in it. This chapter features the plants that attract birds, from towering evergreens and deciduous trees to shrubs, annuals, and perennials.

FORTUNATELY, BIRDS AND GARDENERS are attracted to many of the same plants, or at least to similar ones. In fact, the best species for birds include many beloved garden plants, including dogwoods, crab apples, and viburnums. As a result, it is an easy matter to create an attractive garden that appeals to birds and people alike.

Keep in mind, however, that birds and gardeners make their plant choices for entirely different reasons. While a gardener plants dogwoods and crab apples for their gorgeous spring flowers, birds have their own plans for these trees. To them, the flowers provide an ideal hunting ground for insects, and the fruit offers essential food in fall and winter. Viburnums

Many annuals and perennials, such as purple coneflower (*Echinacea*) and black-eyed Susan (*Rudbeckia*), produce a bounty of seeds that will feed birds well into winter.

To create a garden that attracts songbirds like these chipping sparrows, plant an assortment of trees, shrubs, and vines that offer safe nesting sites and winter cover.

are another case in point. Cultivated forms with showy, fragrant snowball-like blooms are popular garden plants, but birds pass right by them, because the flowers are sterile and don't yield berries. For a bird garden, viburnums with smaller, but fertile, flowers and the added bonus of showy fall fruit are the best choice.

Birds also use plants with evergreen foliage for winter cover, and dense, twiggy growth to provide safe nesting sites and protection from predators. Mixed shrub borders, shade plantings, and even semiwild hedgerows are perfect ways to incorporate these needs into an attractive landscape that will attract birds. (See "Arranging Cover Plants" on page 18 for more ideas on how to incorporate bird-attracting plants into your yard.)

In this chapter, you'll find information on some of the best plants for a bird garden. Before you decide what to plant, though, do some local research on the recommended plants for your area. Nature centers, botanical gardens, wild bird centers, and your local library or extension service office have materials available on trees, shrubs, vines, and flowers that are adapted to your climate and attractive to birds in your region. They also have access to information on the types of habitats that are typically found in your region. You also may find experts at a local nursery or garden center. Many gardeners interested in landscaping for wildlife plant only indigenous species. You can use field guides to identify plants that are native to your area.

feeding the birds

BIRD FEEDING IS A TERRIFIC HOBBY that you can enjoy year-round. But for birds, the seed, suet, and other treats you put out during the winter months can be a lifesaver. Many homeowners feed in summer, too, because it allows them to watch birds from indoors all year. There's nothing quite like watching parent birds introduce their latest batch of babies to your feeders.

A basic seed mix of black-oil sunflower, white proso millet, and safflower seed will attract a wide variety of birds that routinely visit feeders. If you like, you can add specialty items such as niger thistle, which attracts goldfinches, and fine or medium cracked corn, which appeals to species like jays and white-throated sparrows. Wild bird centers will be able to tell you which local species are attracted to the different types of seed mixes they sell.

A mix of black-oil sunflower seed, cracked corn, and millet will attract birds such as towhees, cardinals, and juncos.

To attract the widest variety of birds, use several models of feeders and provide food at various heights. Low platforms attract ground-eating species like juncos and mourning doves and keep the seed dry during inclement weather. You can also spread seed on rocks or even right on the ground. Position feeders in sheltered spots that you can see easily from indoors.

Suet feeders attract woodpeckers, as well as nuthatches, chickadees, and Carolina wrens. Avoid using suet when daytime temperatures are above 70°F, because it can turn rancid. You can buy commercial suet mixes, including ones designed for summer feeding, or you can buy chunks of beef suet at the butcher.

TIPS FOR SUCCESS

If you provide backyard birds with a conventional birdbath, adding a fountain or sprayer will add the sight and sound of moving water and attract even more birds. A garden pond that has a shallow end for bathing and a small fountain or waterfall will attract yet more birds, along with dragonflies, frogs, toads, and other creatures. While you're at it, why not add a bog garden at one end too? You may see robins, phoebes, or barn swallows come and gather mud to make their nests.

Summer feeding has its own rewards. With oranges, bananas, raisins, and apples, you can lure orioles, tanagers, robins, and mockingbirds to your feeders. Cut the fruit in half and hang it on an opened coat hanger, stick it on a tree branch, or fasten it to your feeder. Nectar feeders will attract hummingbirds and orioles in addition to hummingbirds. For more on them, see chapter 3.

Ideally, maintain two or more feeding areas in different parts of your yard—one out in the lawn near a group of evergreens, for example, and another in a shade garden or wooded area. Try to be as consistent as possible in keeping feeders filled: the birds that visit your feeders will come to depend on them daily.

nest boxes and other features for a bird garden

IN ADDITION TO FEEDING BIRDS and growing plants that provide food and cover, there are other steps you can take to make your yard attractive to birds. Consider these options:

PROVIDE NEST BOXES AND PLATFORMS

Putting up nest boxes is another way to attract birds to your yard. Species that use them include bluebirds, tree swallows, wrens, purple martins, tufted titmice, chickadees, nuthatches, and woodpeckers. Platforms or nesting shelves will attract species such as robins, barn swallows, and

Locate birdbaths or other water features where they are easy to fill and clean. A site within view of a window will let you enjoy visitors all year.

phoebes. Put up different types of boxes and hang them in a variety of habitats to attract many species of birds. You can also offer nesting materials, if you like. Hang an old suet feeder or wire basket and fill it with dog or cat hair, short strips of cotton fabric, excelsior, or short (8 inches or less) lengths of string or yarn. Stick to natural, biodegradable materials.

PUT UP ROOSTING BOXES

Many small birds such as chickadees huddle together at night in winter to conserve heat. Specially designed roosting boxes are available at wild bird centers. These feature a hole near the bottom, which prevents heat from escaping, and perches designed so birds don't sit directly over one another. Some models can be turned over and converted to conventional bird houses for summer.

SAVE A SNAG

People usually consider dead and dying trees, called snags, eyesores, but many birds see them as home. So before you remove a tree, stop to consider that you are taking down real estate that woodpeckers and many other birds adore.

Woodpeckers are the major engineers that hollow out nesting cavities in dead trees, but many other species enjoy the cavities they hollow out, including chickadees, nuthatches, wrens, tree swallows, brown creepers, great crested flycatchers, and bluebirds. Birds will also nest in the hollow limbs of venerable old trees like oaks. Dead trees also provide ideal hunting grounds for insects, and many birds use them simply to perch and watch over their territory. The ideal snag is at least 6 inches in diameter and more than 15 feet tall. Leaving a dead tree isn't an option for everyone, but if you can, leave one in your garden. If you want to dress up a dead tree, use it as a trellis. Trumpet vine (*Campsis radicans*) will cover up even a large snag and attract hummingbirds in the process. Dedicated backyard wildlife enthusiasts have even erected snags in their yards in order to enjoy the birds they attract.

Berries that persist on trees and shrubs through the winter provide important food for a variety of birds such as robins, bluebirds, mockingbirds, catbirds, and titmice.

MAKE A DUST BATH

Water isn't the only thing that birds bathe in. Many small songbirds visit dry, dusty sites and "bathe" in them to control parasites. You can add a dust bath to your bird garden by pulverizing the soil in a 1½- to 2-foot-diameter area. Either use a garden fork to dig the soil to between 6 and 8 inches and a hoe to pulverize it, or till the area repeatedly. To pulverize the soil most effectively, work it when it is dry.

trees for a bird garden

TREES ARE THE BACKBONE of a landscape designed to attract birds. Not only do they produce edible seeds and nuts, but they also provide essential hunting grounds for insect eaters. Many birds search the flowers and foliage of trees and eat the insects that they find there. Flycatchers, phoebes, kingbirds, and other species make forays from tree branches to catch nearby flying insects. Trees also provide winter cover, nest sites, and places to hide from predators.

TREES FOR BIRDS

In addition to the trees described in this chapter, the following are also recommended for attracting birds because of the berries, seeds, or nuts they provide, or because of their value as cover. Plants marked with a symbol 🍃 tolerate partial shade.

EVERGREEN TREES

Chamaecyparis spp. Cedars
Pseudotsuga menziesii Douglas fir
Thuja occidentalis American arborvitae
Tsuga Hemlock, especially *T. canadensis* and *T. caroliniana*

DECIDUOUS TREES

Alnus spp. Alders, especially *A. glutinosa* 🍃
Betula spp. Birches, especially *B. lenta*, *B. papyrifera*, *B. occidentalis*, and *B. populifolia*
Carya spp. Hickories

Corylus spp. Hazlenuts, filberts 🍃
Elaeagnus spp. Russian olives, especially *E. angustifolia*, *E. multiflora*, and *E. umbellata* (Note: These can be weedy and have been declared noxious weeds in some states.)
Fagus spp. Beeches
Fraxinus spp. Ashes
Liriodendron tulipifera Tulip tree
Nyssa sylvatica Black gum 🍃
Platanus spp. Sycamores
Populus spp. Poplars or cottonwoods
Sorbus spp. Mountain ashes

FIRS

birds attracted

Many species, including towhees, nuthatches, grosbeaks, chickadees, crossbills, and jays. Blue and sharp-tailed grouse eat the flat needles.

Distinctive and popular, these handsome, densely branched evergreens provide important cover and plentiful seeds for a variety of species. They are pyramidal to columnar in habit and grow slowly to heights of 40 to 100 feet, depending on the species. The seeds are contained in upright cones that appear in summer. In late fall, when they reach maturity, the cones open to scatter seeds that are relished by many kinds of birds. Firs are best suited to regions with cool, humid conditions like those of their mountainous native habitats. White fir (*Abies concolor*), nikko fir (*A. homolepis*), and noble fir (*A. procera*) are all good choices. Balsam fir (*A. balsamea*) and Fraser fir (*A. fraseri*) are also popular.

ABIES SPP.

ZONES:
4–7, depending on the species

culture

Grow firs in moist, well-drained, acid soil. They tolerate light shade, but a site in full sun is best. Mulch the soil with leaves, shredded bark, or wood chips to keep the roots cool and the soil moist.

Abies concolor

MAPLES

birds attracted

Cardinals, grosbeaks, and purple finches eat the seeds. Chickadees, nuthatches, warblers, and other species hunt for insects in the bark and among the leaves and flowers.

Maples produce a bounty of summer seeds for birds, along with nest sites and cover. Birds also hunt for insects among the early spring flowers and summer foliage. These broad-spreading trees have lobed leaves and range in height from 25 to 100 feet at maturity. There are many good species to choose from. Amur maple *(Acer ginnala)* is a good choice for small gardens; red maple *(A. rubrum)* and sugar maple *(A. saccharum)* are large trees for large spaces. Box elder *(A. negundo)* is considered a weed tree in some parts of the country, but produces abundant crops of seeds and is a good choice in the Great Plains and Southwest. Box elder is dioecious, so be sure to buy male and female trees to obtain seeds. Japanese maple *(A. palmatum)* is a fine plant for sites in dappled shade.

ACER SPP.

ZONES:
3–9, depending on the species

culture

In general, maples grow best in rich, moist, well-drained soil and will grow in full sun to half-shade. They require irrigation in areas that receive less than 30 inches of rainfall per year.

Acer concolor

SERVICEBERRIES

birds attracted

Many species eat the berries, including bluebirds, catbirds, grosbeaks, jays, mockingbirds, robins, thrushes, woodpeckers, towhees, orioles, tanagers, and cedar waxwings. The spring flowers also attract insects that many birds appreciate.

Also called shadbush, shadblow, and juneberry, these small, deciduous trees produce clouds of tiny white flowers in spring. The flowers are followed by small purplish fruit that attracts both birds and humans. Many species make ideal additions to bird gardens and are especially effective planted on the edges of woodlands, in shrub borders, and along streams and ponds. Plants range in size from 10 to 20 feet. Downy serviceberry (*A. arborea*), saskatoon serviceberry (*A. alnifolia*), and Allegheny serviceberry (*A. laevis*) are good choices. Shadblow serviceberry (*A. canadensis*) is a shrubby, 6- to 20-foot species that spreads by suckers. Running serviceberry (*A. stolonifera*) is a stoloniferous shrub that forms thickets.

AMELANCHIER SPP.

ZONES:
4–8, depending on the species

culture

Serviceberries will grow in ordinary garden soil but prefer moist, well-drained, acid conditions. They tolerate partial shade. Mulch to keep the soil moist. Water during very dry spells.

Saskatoon serviceberry (*Amelanchier alnifolia*) produces clusters of tiny white flowers followed by round purplish blue berries. This is the variety 'Thiessen'.

HACKBERRIES

birds attracted

Bluebirds, fox sparrows, flickers and woodpeckers, cardinals, mockingbirds, thrashers, thrushes, quail, phoebes, towhees, and titmice are among the birds that eat the berries. Many species also nest in the branches.

Although often overlooked as ornamentals, hackberries make valuable additions to any bird garden because of their small (1/3 inch) blackish purple fruit. They are ideal trees to plant in difficult sites because they tolerate a wide range of soil conditions, as well as air pollution. Use these large 40- to 60-foot trees as background plants, behind shrub borders, or to provide shade on a tough site. Common hackberry (*Celtis occidentalis*) and sugar hackberry (*C. laevigata*) are two good choices.

CELTIS SPP.

ZONES: 3–9, depending on the species

culture

Hackberries tolerate acid or alkaline soil that ranges from somewhat wet to very dry, although they do best in rich, moist soil. Plant them in full sun.

Celtis occidentalis

DOGWOODS

birds attracted

More than ninety species of birds eat dogwood berries, including catbirds, mockingbirds, robins, thrushes, woodpeckers, vireos, white-throated sparrows, song sparrows, bluebirds, cardinals, and kingbirds. Many warblers and other birds also hunt for insects among dogwood branches and in the furrows of the bark.

Dogwoods are excellent plants for a bird garden because of their tasty berries that provide food in summer, fall, and winter. All bear spring flowers with showy white, or sometimes pink, bracts. The flowers are followed by bright fruit and stunning fall color, making these trees outstanding specimen plants or lovely additions to tree and shrub borders. Flowering dogwood (*Cornus florida*) is a beloved ornamental with clusters of shiny red berries in fall. Kousa or Japanese dogwood (*C. kousa*) bears blooms slightly later and has red, raspberry-like fruits. Both are small trees ranging from 20 to 30 feet. Pacific dogwood (*C. nuttalli*) is a large tree (to 75 feet) with red or orange summer-to-fall fruits. It is best grown in the Pacific Northwest. (For information on shrubby dogwoods, see "*Cornus* spp." on page 68.)

CORNUS SPP.

ZONES:
5–9, depending on the species; *C. nuttalli* is hardy in Zones 7–9.

culture

Dogwoods grow well in most good garden soils, but prefer well-drained, acid soil that is rich in organic matter. Mulch to keep the soil moist and cool. Partial shade is ideal, although dogwoods will tolerate full sun.

Kousa dogwood (*Cornus kousa*) features showy, raspberry-like fruit on long stalks.

HAWTHORNS

birds attracted

Jays, mockingbirds, robins, and grosbeaks are among the birds that eat hawthorn berries. Mourning doves and cardinals are two of the species that nest among the thorny branches. Many species also search for insects among the leaves and flowers.

These small trees produce clusters of white spring flowers followed by clusters of small berries that attract a number of birds. Their branches are generally armed with stout, sharp thorns, which provide excellent protection for nesting birds. Cockspur hawthorn (*Crataegus crus-galli*) and Lavalle hawthorn (*C. x lavallei*) bear half-inch fruit; Washington hawthorn (*C. phaenopyrum*) is an especially good choice because of its smaller, quarter-inch fruits, which are eaten by more species. Hummingbirds also visit its flowers. Use these plants for barrier plantings, as well as tree and shrub borders.

CRATAEGUS SPP.

ZONES:
3–9, depending on the species

culture

Hawthorns grow well in ordinary to poor garden soil. They are especially suited for alkaline soil and withstand drought and harsh weather. Plant in full sun. Avoid planting them near walkways because of their thorns; prune off branches or thorns that might pose a hazard for garden visitors.

Washington hawthorn (*Crataegus phaenopyrum*).

HOLLIES

birds attracted

Bluebirds, robins, waxwings, catbirds, and mockingbirds are among the species that enjoy the berries, which generally last well into winter.

The round, red, pea-sized berries of hollies provide important fall-to-early-spring food for many kinds of birds. Trees in this genus, which range from 20 to 50 feet in height, also provide important cover because of their glossy, evergreen leaves. Use hollies as specimen plants and in tree and shrub borders. American holly and longstalk holly (*Ilex pedunculosa*) are good choices. English holly (*I. aquifolium*) is a good choice south of Zone 7, although it does not grow well in areas with hot, dry summers. (For information on shrub hollies, see *"Ilex* spp." on page 69.)

ILEX SPP.

ZONES:
5–9

culture

Plant hollies in partial shade in acid, loamy soil that is well drained. Protect plants from wind. Spring planting of balled-and-burlapped or container-grown plants is recommended. Be sure to plant both male and female plants of any species you grow to ensure berries; one male will pollinate three female plants.

American holly

JUNIPERS

birds attracted

The berries provide important winter food for a variety of species, including bluebirds, catbirds, crossbills, purple finches, grosbeaks, jays, mockingbirds, quail, and thrushes. Native sparrows, robins, and mockingbirds often nest in junipers.

The round, blue, berrylike fruits of many junipers and the dense, evergreen branches covered with scalelike needles attract a variety of birds. Although many shrub-sized junipers are available, trees in this genus are preferable because they provide nest sites and winter cover. Eastern red cedar (*Juniperus virginiana*) and Rocky Mountain juniper or Western red cedar (*J. scopulorum*) are both good choices that range from 40 to 75 feet in height.

JUNIPERUS SPP.

ZONES:
3–10, depending
on the species

culture

Plant junipers in full sun in a site with well-drained soil. They will grow in evenly moist, well-drained soils and also endure dry, rocky sites as well as wind and drought.

Junipers bear abundant crops of berries that many birds eat in winter, when other foods are scarce.

CRAB APPLE, APPLES

birds attracted

Woodpeckers and flickers, robins, mockingbirds, catbirds, and grosbeaks all eat crab apples.

Crab apples produce a glorious spring display of white or pink flowers followed by berries that a variety of birds savor. These small, round-headed trees, which range from 15 to 30 feet in height, also offer secure nest sites. Many species hunt for insects among the leaves and branches of both crab apples and apples. Hummingbirds visit the flowers. The best crab apples for feeding birds bear small fruit that persists on the trees into winter. See "Small-Fruited Crab Apples" below for a list of species and cultivars to consider.

MALUS SPP.

ZONES:
3 or 4–8, depending on the species

culture

Grow crab apples in moist, well-drained soil and full sun. They tolerate acid to somewhat alkaline soils.

Malus crab apples are small trees that produce clouds of white flowers in late spring followed by small dark red berries.

SMALL-FRUITED CRAB APPLES

Many popular crab apples feature fruit that is far too large for birds to fit in their mouths. You can provide a veritable feast that lasts well into winter by planting cultivars that bear fruit under a half-inch in diameter. (Birds generally wait to eat the fruit until it has been softened by winter freezes.) The following crab apples all bear fruit smaller than that—from a quarter- to a third-inch in diameter—that even small birds can enjoy with ease. In addition, all the cultivars listed are also disease-resistant.

Species crab apples include carmine crab apple (*Malus* x *atrosanguinea*), Japanese flowering crab apple (*M. floribunda*), tea crab apple (*M. hupehensis*), and Sargent crab apple (*M. sargentii*).

Cultivars include 'Autumn Glory', 'Autumn Treasure', 'Donald Wyman', 'Fiesta', 'Firebelle', 'Firebrand', 'Fireburst', 'Golden Dream', 'Cornell', 'Katherine', 'Little Troll', 'Matador', 'Molten Lava', 'Pagoda', 'Peter Pan', 'Sea Foam', 'Sinai Fire', 'Wildfire', 'Woven Gold', and 'Zumirang'.

MULBERRIES

birds attracted

Nearly sixty species of birds relish mulberries, including scarlet tanagers, orioles, cardinals, phainopepla, woodpeckers, bluebirds, and waxwings.

Mulberries are often first on the list of undesirable weed trees, but that's not where birds would rank them. The succulent purple-black berries, which are borne only on female trees, provide a bounty of summer food for birds and a variety of other wild creatures—including box turtles. They range from 30 to 50 feet in height and also offer safe cover and nest sites. Use them in wild areas, hedgerows, or as background plants. Common mulberry (*Morus alba*), red mulberry (*M. rubra*), and Texas mulberry (*M. microphylla*) are species to look for. Be sure to select a fruiting, female plant, not one of the new male, nonfruiting cultivars.

MORUS SPP.

ZONES:
4–9, depending on the species

culture

Grow mulberries in almost any soil in full sun.

White mulberry (*Morus alba*).

SPRUCES

birds attracted

Nuthatches, crossbills, chickadees, pine siskins, and grosbeaks all eat spruce seeds.

Spruces are pyramidal evergreens that provide important winter cover as well as edible seeds. Grouse eat the needles. Spruce trees range from 60 to over 100 feet in height. Their sharp needles and densely branching habit make them ideal nest sites. Use these large plants as windbreaks, specimens, or as backdrops for other shrubs and trees. Norway spruce (*Picea abies*), Serbian spruce (*P. omorika*), and Colorado spruce (*P. pungens*) are three popular species.

PICEA SPP.

ZONES:
2–7, depending on the species

culture

Plant spruces in full sun to light shade. They will tolerate a range of soils, but require evenly moist conditions. Avoid soil that is too dry or too wet. Also avoid exposed sites where they will be subjected to drying winds.

Norway spruce (*Picea abies* 'Acrocona' shown here) bears 6-inch-long cones that provide seeds for many birds in winter. The dense branches offer winter cover as well.

PINES

birds attracted

Many species, including grosbeaks, jays, nuthatches, pine siskins, titmice, towhees, woodpeckers, crossbills, and Clark's nutcrackers eat the seeds.

These magnificent evergreens provide cover, winter protection, and nest sites, as well as edible seeds and sap. Several species of grouse, as well as wild turkeys, eat the needles. Most are large trees, from 60 to 100 feet at maturity. Dwarf and slow-growing cultivars of many species are available. There are species for gardens in every part of the country, including eastern white pine (*Pinus strobus*), jack pine (*P. banksiana*), and red pine (*P. resinosa*) for the Midwest and East. Longleaf and loblolly pines (*P. palustris* and *P. taeda*) are suitable for the Southeast. For prairie states west to the Pacific, species include lodgepole pine (*P. contorta*), limber pine (*P. jlexilis*), ponderosa pine (*P. ponderosa*), and Mexican pinyon (*P. cembroides*).

PINUS SPP.

ZONES:
2–10, depending on the species

culture

Most pines grow well in light to average, well-drained soil and full sun. Some species tolerate dry soil. Use these evergreens to create windbreaks to block prevailing winter winds. They also make fine specimen trees.

White pine (*Pinus strobus*) can be used in windbreaks, and it also provides food and nest sites for a variety of species.

CHERRIES

birds attracted

More than eighty species of birds eat cherries, including robins, bluebirds, woodpeckers, catbirds, thrushes, cardinals, blackbirds, tanagers, jays, and orioles.

As anyone who raises sweet cherries (*Prunus avium*) or tart cherries (*P. cerasus*) for pies and jellies knows, birds relish these glossy, round red fruits. In addition to cultivated cherries, they also gobble up the summer fruit of a variety of wild cherries, including pin cherry (*P. pensylvanica*), wild black cherry (*P. serotina*), and chokecherry (*P. virginiana*). In desert and mountain regions, bitter cherry (*P. emarginata*) and western chokecherry (*P. virginiana* var. *demissa*) make good additions to bird gardens. Sand cherry (*P. besseyi*) is a suckering shrub that reaches 6 feet and bears purple-black fruit. In general, cherries are small trees, from 15 to 40 feet in height, that are effective in shrub borders and hedgerows.

PRUNUS SPP.

ZONES:
5–10, depending on the species

culture

Plant cherries in full sun and evenly moist, well-drained soil. Mulch them to keep the soil cool and moist, and water deeply during periods of drought.

Black Cherry tree (*Prunus serotina*).

OAKS

birds attracted

Jays are major acorn consumers, but many other birds will also eat them, including chickadees, grouse, bobwhites and quail, grosbeaks, and cardinals. Many of these species also hunt for insects among the branches. In western states, acorn woodpeckers collect and store vast quantities of the nuts.

Oaks are majestic trees that produce acorns and also provide nesting sites. There are about 450 species of oaks, ranging from mid-sized 40- or 50-foot trees to giants that exceed 100 feet. The region you live in is the best indicator of which species to plant. For eastern gardens, white oak (*Quercus alba*), scarlet oak (*Q. coccínea*), bur oak (*Q. macrocarpa*), and pin oak (*Q. palustris*) are nice choices. Southeastern gardeners can grow laurel oak (*Q. laurifolia*), blackjack oak (*Q. marilandica*), willow oak (*Q. phellos*), and live oak (*Q. virginiana*). Bur oak (*Q. macrocarpa*) is a good selection for the Great Plains, as are shingle oak (*Q. imbricaria*) and blackjack oak (*Q. marilandica*). Gardeners in western regions can consider Gambel oak (*Q. gambeli*) and Rocky Mountain white oak (*Q. utahensis*). In Zones 8 and warmer along the Pacific Coast, canyon live oak (*Q. chrysolepis*), *California black oak (Q. kelloggii)*, and valley oak (*Q. lobata*) are the best options.

QUERCUS SPP.

ZONES:
4–10, depending
on the species

culture

Oaks grow best in full sun, although most will tolerate some partial shade. Rich, deep soil is ideal. Mulch oak trees, but avoid grade changes, trenching, and soil compaction in the root zone, which can kill them. Transplanting can be tricky, but fortunately researchers have recently developed new techniques for growing oaks in containers, and more species can be successfully transplanted than ever before.

Both the acorns of oaks, such as this red oak (*Quercus rubra*), and the insects among the branches attract a variety of birds.

shrubs and brambles for a bird garden

EVEN GARDENERS WHO DON'T HAVE SPACE for more than one full-size tree on their property can find room for an assortment of smaller shrubs or a thicket of bramble fruit. For best results, plant several different shrubs—either individually or in masses—and combine them with larger trees to create dense plantings that provide cover as well as food. You can also underplant existing trees with berry-producing shrubs to create a food-rich woodland or shade planting. Shrubs also work well when incorporated into perennial gardens.

SHRUBS FOR BIRDS

In addition to the shrubs and brambles described in this chapter, the following also are recommended for attracting birds because of the berries or seeds they provide. Plants marked with a symbol 🍃 tolerate partial shade.

Arbutus spp. Strawberry tree, madrone, including *A. unedo* and *A. menziesii* 🍃

Arctostapbylos spp. Manzanitas and bearberries, including *A. uva-ursi*, *A. glauca*, *A. manzanita*, and *A. tomentosa* 🍃

Empetrum spp. Crowberries

Euonymus alatus Winged euonymus 🍃

Lindera benzoin Spicebush 🍃

Mahonia aquifolium Oregon grape holly

Myrica spp. Bayberry and waxberries, including *M. pensylvanica*, *M. californica*, and *M. cerifera* 🍃

Eyracantha spp. Pyracantha or firethorn, especially *P. coccinea* 🍃

Rhamnus spp. Buckthorns, including *R. cathartica*, *R. alnifolia*, and *F. californica* 🍃

Ribes spp. Gooseberries and currants 🍃

Shepherdia spp. Buffaloberries, especially *S. canadensis* and *S. argentea*

Symphoricarpus spp. Snowberries and coralberries, especially *S. albus*, *S. occidentalis*, and *S. orbiculatus* 🍃

Taxus spp. Yews 🍃

Red elderberry (*Sambucus racemosa*) produces clusters of yellowish white flowers in late spring followed by showy round red berries in late summer.

SUMACS

birds attracted

Since sumac fruits persist on the plants into winter, they are an important source of food. More than ninety-five species of birds have been observed eating them, including towhees, woodpeckers and flickers, chickadees, robins, vireos, thrushes, catbirds, wild turkeys, and bobwhites.

Sumacs are large shrubs or small trees that produce featherlike compound leaves and cone-shaped clusters of berrylike fruit that are an important source of winter food for birds. They are effective in wild gardens or on banks; since most spread rapidly by suckers, it's best to avoid sites where spreading would be a problem. Staghorn sumac (*Rhus typhina*) is a 10- to 30-foot shrub or small tree and the best garden ornamental. Fragrant sumac (*R. aromatica*) and flameleaf or shining sumac (*R. copallina*) are other species to consider. Lemonade sumac (*R. integrifolia*) is a California native that can be grown in Zones 9 and 10.

RHUS SPP.

ZONES:
3–9, depending on the species

culture

Sumacs will grow in any garden soil in full sun. They can also be planted in difficult sites, including dry sand and rocky hillsides.

Sumacs, such as this *Rhus typhina*, are best suited to wild gardens. Their conelike fruit clusters are attractive to more than ninety-five species of birds.

ROSES

birds attracted

A variety of birds will nest in the thorny branches of large shrub roses, including cardinals, sparrows, towhees, and indigo buntings. These birds, plus thrushes, robins, bluebirds, vireos, quail, and a host of other species, eat the berries, especially in late winter when food is scarce.

Roses are, of course, one of America's most beloved garden flowers, but pampered hybrid teas are not the best roses for a bird garden. To welcome birds, look for shrub roses that bear small hips that they can eat easily. The berries provide important winter food, and the dense branches of these 5- to 15-foot plants provide cover and nest sites as well. Tough, vigorous, disease-resistant plants are also important, because spraying chemical controls will endanger the birds. Shrub roses are effective in perennial and shrub borders, as well as cottage and wild gardens. Multiflora rose (*Rosa multiflora*) bears an abundance of small hips, but is a noxious weed found in many parts of the country because birds have spread the seed far and wide. The large hips of rugosa roses (*R. rugosa*) are showy, but generally too large for birds to eat. Better choices include Carolina or pasture rose (*R. carolina*), meadow rose (*R. blanda*), Cherokee rose (*R. laevigata*), nootka rose (*R. nutkana*), Virginia rose (*R. virginiana*), and prairie wild rose (*R. arkansana*).

ROSA SPP.

ZONES:
3–9, depending on the species

culture

Plant roses in full sun with well-drained, rich soil.

Cherokee rose (*Rosa laevigata*).

BRAMBLES

birds attracted

Nearly 150 species of birds eat bramble berries, including bluebirds, cardinals, catbirds, grosbeaks, jays, mockingbirds, orioles, phoebes, robins, sparrows, tanagers, vireos, waxwings, and woodpeckers.

It comes as no surprise that birds eat the fruit of blackberries, raspberries, and other brambles, including tayberries, wineberries, boysenberries, and loganberries. In fact, if you grow any of these crops for your own use, you'll have to fight the birds for them. Brambles also produce dense thickets of thorny canes that provide excellent cover and nesting sites as well. If you protect your bramble crops with netting, plant extras for the birds to enjoy. Brambles are ideal in hedgerows and wild gardens. Ask your local extension service to recommend the best bramble crops for your region.

RUBUS SPP.

ZONES:
3–10, depending on the species

culture

Grow brambles in full sun in rich, well-drained soil.

Brambles such as these *Rubus canadensis* 'Perron's Black' raspberries are as attractive to people as they are to birds.

ELDERBERRIES

birds attracted

Elderberries provide a feast of summer fruit for 120 species of birds or more, including bluebirds, grosbeaks, sparrows, phainopepla, thrashers, catbirds, vireos, finches, doves, woodpeckers, and flickers.

Elderberries bear flat clusters of small white flowers in late spring, followed by large clusters of red or black berrylike fruits. These shrubs or small trees range in height from 6 to as much as 45 feet and have handsome, compound leaves. Elderberries prefer moist soil and are ideal for pond edges, drainage ditches, and other boggy areas. They can also be used in shrub borders and along woodland edges. American elderberry *(Sambucus canadensis)* grows wild throughout the eastern half of the country. Blue elderberry *(S. caerulea)* is a Pacific Coast native. European elder *(S. nigra)* and European red elder *(S. racemosa)* are also suitable.

SAMBUCUS SPP.

ZONES:
4–9

culture

Elderberries are easy to grow in nearly any type of soil, although they grow best in moist sites. If these sprawling plants become overgrown, simply cut them to the ground and they'll quickly regrow.

BLUEBERRIES

birds attracted

Bluebirds, robins, orioles, titmice, towhees, jays, thrushes, tanagers, and thrashers are among the many birds that eat blueberries.

Blueberries are another cultivated crop that are every bit as popular with birds as they are with people. They bear urn-shaped flowers in spring, followed by many-seeded berries. The plants range from 8 inches to 18 feet or more. The most common blueberries are lowbush blueberry (*Vaccinium angustifolium*), highbush blueberry (*V. corymbosum*), and rabbiteye blueberry (*V. ashei*). Several other members of the genus produce berries that birds relish, including dryland blueberry (*V. pallidum*), common deerberry (*V. stamineum*), and mountain cranberry (*V. vitis idaea*). Ask your local extension service to recommend blueberries for your area. If you protect blueberry crops with netting or cages, add extra plants for birds. They make ideal additions to foundation plantings, shrub and tree borders, and mixed plantings of shrubs and perennials.

VACCINIUM SPP.

ZONES:
2–9, depending on the species

culture

Blueberries require acid soil that is moist but well drained. Grow them in full sun for best fruit production, but they will also grow well in partial shade.

VIBURNUMS

birds attracted

Robins, grosbeaks, catbirds, thrushes, thrashers, towhees, cardinals, cuckoos, and bluebirds are among the birds that enjoy viburnum berries.

Viburnum is a large genus of showy ornamental shrubs, a few of which can be limbed up to create small trees. They are either deciduous or evergreen, and they range in height from 4 to 30 feet. The clusters of white spring flowers are followed by fleshy, berrylike fruits in red, yellow, blue, or black. On some species, the birds gobble up the fruit soon after they are ripe in late summer or fall; other species, perhaps less palatable, remain on the bushes into winter and early spring, where they provide much-needed food when other sources are scarce. Use viburnums along woodland edges, in shrub and tree borders, and in foundation plantings. Snowball-type viburnums bear round clusters of sterile flowers and do not produce fruit. Red-fruited viburnums include linden viburnum (*Viburnum dilatatum*), European cranberry-bush viburnum (*V. opulus*), siebold viburnum (*V. sieboldii*), American cranberry-bush viburnum (*V. trilobum*), and Wright viburnum (*V. wrightii*). Viburnums with blue, blue-black, or black fruit include mapleleaf viburnum (*V. acerifolium*), withe-rod viburnum (*V. cassinoides*), arrowwood viburnum (*V. dentatum*), wayfaring tree (*V. lantana*), nannyberry viburnum (*V. lentago*), black haw (*V. prunifolium*), and Southern black haw (*V. rufidulum*). Yellow-fruited viburnums are also available, including *V. opulus* 'Xanthocarpum', *V. sargentii* 'Flavum', and *V. dilatatum* 'Xanthocarpum'.

VIBURNUM SPP.

ZONES:
3–10, depending
on the species

culture

Plant viburnums in full sun and evenly moist, well-drained soil that is slightly acid. Mapleleaf viburnum (*V. acerifolium*) and withe-rod viburnum (*V. cassinoides*) are suitable for shady sites.

American cranberry-bush viburnum (*Viburnum trilobum*) bears white spring flowers followed by red fruit that matures in midsummer and persists on the plants well into winter.

flowers, grasses, and vines for a bird garden

TREES AND SHRUBS that provide food and cover are by far the most important plants in a garden designed to attract songbirds. However, a flower bed or a meadow garden planted with annuals, perennials, and grasses that produce an abundance of edible seeds is a beneficial addition. Flower seeds attract a variety of seed-eating birds, including cardinals, sparrows, finches, towhees, thrashers, buntings, and juncos. Be sure to include some hummingbird plants, too.

VINES FOR BIRDS

Several species of vines provide berries that birds eat, and their tangled stems create ideal nest sites and cover.

Grapes (*Vitis* spp.) are probably the most important vines for feeding birds. They are popular with many species, including bluebirds, cardinals, jays, and thrashers. Birds eat cultivated grapes as well as wild species, such as summer or pigeon grape (*V. aestivalis*), winter grape (*V. vulpina*), fox grape (*V. labrusca*), riverbank grape (*V. riparia*), canyon grape (*V. arizonica*), and California grape (*V. californica*). Virginia creeper, or woodbine (*Parthenocissus quinquefolia*), also provides berries for birds, as do the greenbriers or catbriers (*Smilax* spp.) and American bittersweet (*Celastris scandens*). (Beware of Chinese bittersweet, *C. orbiculatus*, which is more rampant and has become a noxious weed in the Northeast.)

Sunflowers are easy to grow and will produce an abundance of seeds for birds. Let birds eat them right in the garden or dry the flowers upside down and save them for winter feeding. You can remove the seeds from the central flower or simply hang the flowers up and let the birds remove them for you.

Use the list of annuals, perennials, and grasses on pages 82, 84, and 86, respectively, to get started. All thrive in full sun in average to rich, well-drained soil. Seeds from these plants will provide food from summer into winter. In order to promote seed production, do not deadhead the flowers. Leave the plants standing in the garden after fall frost, and allow birds to feast on the seeds through winter. Cut the plants back in spring.

Plants marked with a butterfly symbol 🦋 also attract butterflies.

Plants marked with a hummingbird symbol 🐦 attract hummingbirds.

ANNUALS AND BIENNIALS

Alcea rosea Garden hollyhock

Amaranthus caudatus Love-lies-bleeding

Amaranthus hybridus var. *erythrostachys* Prince's feather

Briza maxima Quaking grass

Calendula officinalis Pot marigold

Callistephus chinensis China asters

Centaurea cyanus Bachelor's button

Consolida ambigua Larkspur

Coreopsis tinctoria Golden coreopsis

Cosmos bipinnatus and *C. sulphureus* Cosmos

Dianthus barbatus Sweet William

Eschscholzia californica California poppy

Helianthus annuus Common sunflowers

Nigella damascena Love-in-a-mist

Papaver spp. Poppies, especially *P. rhoeas*, *P. nudicaule*, and *P. somniferum*

Phlox drummondi Annual phlox

Tagetes spp. Marigolds

Tithonia rotundifolia Mexican sunflower (Y1)

Zinnia spp. Zinnias, including *Z. officinalis* and *Z. elegans*

Love-lies-bleeding (*Amaranthus caudatus*).

Larkspur (*Consolida ambigua*).

California poppy (*Eschscholzia californica*).

PERENNIALS

Achillea spp. Yarrow

Aquilegia spp. Columbines

Asclepias spp. Milkweeds, including
    A. incarnata (swamp milkweed) and
    A. tuberosa (butterfly weed) (W)

Aster spp. Asters

Coreopsis lanceolata Lance-leaved
    coreopsis

Coreopsis spp. Coreopsis, tickseed

Daucus carota Queen Anne's lace

Echinacea spp. Coneflowers, including
    E. purpurea (purple coneflower) and
    E. pallida (pale coneflower)

Echinops ritro Globe thistle

Eupatorium spp. Boneset, Joe-Pye weed

Fragaria virginiana Wild strawberry

Helianthus spp. Perennial sunflowers

Heliopsis helianthoides Sunflower
    heliopsis

Liatris spp. Blazing star

Papaver orientale Oriental poppy

Ratibida pinnata Gray-headed
    coneflower

Rudbeckia spp. Coneflowers, black-eyed
    Susans

Silphium lanciniatum Compass plant

Solidago spp. Goldenrods

Vernonia noveboracensis Ironweed

Viola spp. Violets

Yarrow (*Achillea millefolium* 'Little Moonshine').

Columbine (*Aquilegia canadensis* 'Little Lanterns').

Butterfly weed
(*Asclepias tuberosa*).

Wild strawberry
(*Fragaria virginiana*).

Black-eyed Susan
(*Rudbeckia hirta*).

GRASSES

Many grasses produce abundant seeds that birds eat. The list below includes just a few native species. Many ornamental grasses that are not native also produce an abundant harvest of seeds. Birds will also appreciate cultivated plots of millet, wheat, or oats. Weedy areas often support foxtails (*Setaria* spp.) and other grasses that birds enjoy.

Andropogon gerardii Big bluestem

Andropogon virginicus Broomsedge bluestem

Bouteloua curtipendula Sideoats grama grass

Buchloe dactyloides Buffalo grass

Chasmanthium latifolium Northern sea oats

Deschampsia caespitosa Tufted hairgrass

Elymus spp., including *E. canadensis* (Canada wild rye) and *E. villosus* (slender wild rye)

Koeleria cristata June grass

Panicum virgatum Switch grass

Schizachynum scoparium Little bluestem

Sorgastrum nutans Indian grass

Switch grass (*Panicum virgatum* 'Squaw').

Northern sea oats
(*Chasmanthium latifolium*).

Native grasses are ideal for planting in prairie or meadow gardens, where their seeds will provide food for birds from summer through winter. Use nonnative ornamental grasses as seed sources in flower and shrub borders.

bird profiles

ON THE FOLLOWING PAGES you will find brief profiles for 30 common backyard birds. Each species profile includes information describing that bird, its field marks, sounds, habitat preferences, and what foods and features may attract it to your yard (in addition to the plants mentioned elsewhere in the book). A photograph accompanies each profile, but some of the individuals you encounter may appear slightly different because of the effects of molting, age, weather, and light conditions. The birds are listed in taxonomic order, which is the organization ornithologists and other scientists use to group related bird species and families. Most bird guides are based on taxonomic order.

KEY TO RANGE MAPS

SUMMER RANGE

WINTER RANGE

YEAR-ROUND RANGE

– – – APPROXIMATE LIMITS OF SUMMER RANGE

– – – APPROXIMATE LIMITS OF WINTER RANGE

– – – APPROXIMATE LIMITS OF YEAR-ROUND RANGE

downy

hairy

DRYOBATES
PUBESCENS (left)
SIZE: 6½"–6¾"

DRYOBATES
VILLOSUS (right)
SIZE: 9"–9¼"

HAIRY WOODPECKER
DOWNY WOODPECKER

Remembering this phrase can help you separate these two look-alike woodpeckers: "Downy is dinky, hairy is huge." This refers both to the birds' respective body sizes and the relative length of their bills.

hairy

downy

field marks

Both species are mainly black on the back and white below. Hairy woodpeckers show an obvious white patch in the middle of the black back and unmarked white outer tail feathers. The hairy's bill is longer than its head is wide. The downy's bill is shorter than its head is wide, and its outer tail feathers are marked with black. Males of both species have a red patch at the back of the head.

sounds

DOWNY: a rapid whinny dropping in pitch. Call is a flat *pik!*
HAIRY: loud rattle call does not descend in pitch. Call is a sharp, loud *peek!*

habitat

Both species prefer forests, parks with large trees, and backyards. Hairy woodpeckers prefer older, larger trees than downies do.

backyard

Both species commonly visit feeders for sunflower seed, suet, suet dough, peanuts, and fruit bits.

COLAPTES
AURATUS
SIZE: 12½"

NORTHERN FLICKER

A woodpecker that does much of its foraging on the ground, the northern flicker comes in two color variations: yellow-shafted and red-shafted. The smaller gilded flicker is a separate species with a limited range in the desert Southwest.

field marks

The northern flicker has many field marks: an obvious white rump and brown back, a buff breast with black spots, and a black half-collar. The male has a mustache (red in red-shafted and black in yellow-shafted). The female does not have facial markings.

sounds

Flickers give a variety of calls: a loud, ringing *week-week-week-week-week*. **Also** *klee-ear!* And *flicker-flicker-flicker*, for which the birds are named.

habitat

Open woodlands, forests, parks, and towns with large trees. Flickers often forage on the ground for ants, using their tongue to extract them from anthills.

backyard

Flickers may visit feeders for suet, suet dough, peanuts, and fruit, but they are more likely to forage on open lawns and open ground for ants.

PERISOREUS
CANADENSIS
SIZE: 11½"

CANADA JAY

Known as the "camp robber" for its bold food-grabbing ways, the Canada jay is a chunky bird with a stout bill and crestless head. It inhabits the woods of the far North and higher elevations in western mountains.

field marks

This jay is dark gray above and pale gray below, with a dark hood across the back of the head. It has a pale forehead and a large dark eye. The bill appears short for a jay.

sounds

Call is a soft, two-noted *wee-ohh!* Also utters other short raspy notes.

habitat

Northern boreal forests of fir and spruce. Common near campgrounds, parks, trails.

backyard

Will visit backyards for suet and meat scraps. Tame Canada jays are common at woodland resorts, ski lodges, and campgrounds.

CYANOCITTA
CRISTATA
SIZE: 11"

BLUE JAY

This large, bold, and noisy bird is often found in loose flocks. Like other members of the corvid family (crows, jays, etc.), it has a reputation for intelligence and adaptability, eating a wide variety of foods and storing surplus food for later consumption.

field marks

This is the only large, crested, blue-colored bird in the East. The crest and back are blue, the face and belly white. Blue jays flash white wing bars and outer tail feathers in flight. They are similar to the Steller's jays of the West, which are slightly larger and darker overall, lacking any white in the wings or tail.

sounds

A harsh, scolding *jaay!* Also gives a variety of unusual calls, including bell-like whistles, rusty squeaks, and toots. Will imitate the calls of hawks.

habitat

Any wooded habitat (especially those with nut-bearing trees), backyards, parks.

backyard

Blue jays eat almost anything at bird feeders, including peanuts, suet, suet dough, sunflower seeds, fruit, and cracked corn. They also visit birdbaths. They will scream like a hawk to scare other birds away from feeders.

carolina   black-capped

POECILE
CAROLINENSIS (left)
SIZE: 4¾"

POECILE
ATRICAPILLUS (right)
SIZE: 5¼"

CAROLINA CHICKADEE
BLACK-CAPPED CHICKADEE

These two small, charming woodland sprites are nearly identical in appearance. Inquisitive by nature, they are often the first birds to visit a new feeder in the backyard.

carolina

black-capped

field marks

A dark cap and throat are offset by white cheeks. Both species show a grayish body with varying amounts of white in the wing bars. Carolinas are cleaner looking and slightly smaller. These birds are best separated by range or voice.

sounds

Both species say *chickadee-dee-dee*, but the black-capped's voice is lower and hoarser than the Carolina's. In spring and summer, the Carolina's song is four sweet notes: *fee-bee, fee-bay*. The black-capped's song is two notes: *fee-bee!*

habitat

Mixed woodlands with large trees, parks, backyards. In winter both species will join other small songbirds to form mixed-species feeding flocks.

backyard

Chickadees visit feeders for a variety of foods: sunflower, suet, peanut butter, peanuts, fruit. They use nest boxes to nest and roost, and they visit birdbaths.

TUFTED TITMOUSE

BAEOLOPHUS BICOLOR

SIZE: 6¼"

In the eastern United States and parts of southeastern Canada, the tufted titmouse may be the most avid visitor to bird-feeding stations. Along with the chickadees, this resident species boldly investigates newly placed feeders, becoming one of the first wild birds to key in on a new food source.

field marks

The tufted titmouse is gray overall and paler below with a crested head. It has a dark eye on a plain face and buffy flanks.

sounds

Song is *peter-peter-peter*. Also utters a variety of call notes and scolds.

habitat

Deciduous woods, parks, woodlots, and backyards.

backyard

Titmice visit feeders for sunflower seed and hearts, peanut butter, peanut bits, and suet and suet dough. They also visit water features to drink and bathe. They may use nest boxes placed in appropriate habitat.

SITTA
CAROLINENSIS
SIZE: 5¾"

WHITE-BREASTED NUTHATCH

Nuthatches climb around on trees gleaning insects from bark and using their chisel-like bills to open seeds and nuts, which they wedge into bark crevices. The white-breasted is the most common backyard visitor among our nuthatches.

field marks

As its name suggests, the white-breasted nuthatch is white below. Its back is solid gray. Its face is also white, with a black crown and nape. The smaller but similar red-breasted nuthatch has a white eyebrow, black eye line, and rusty breast and belly.

sounds

Song is a rapid series of nasal *ank* notes. Call is a single *ank*.

habitat

Forests, open mixed woods, orchards, parks, and shade trees in suburban backyards.

backyard

Nuthatches readily visit feeders for sunflower seeds, suet and suet dough, peanuts, peanut butter, mealworms, and fruit bits. They also visit water features to drink and bathe. They may use nest boxes placed in wooded habitat.

THRYOTHORUS LUDOVICIANUS

SIZE: 5½"

CAROLINA WREN

Usually heard before it is seen, this wren is a year-round resident throughout its range, where it prefers to live near human habitation.

field marks

This wren is rich brown above and warm tan below with a bold white eyebrow and a striped brown tail that is often cocked upward. It is larger than the house wren, the other widespread backyard wren of the East.

sounds

Very vocal year-round. Primary song is a loud, ringing *teakettle, teakettle, teakettle!* Mated pairs stay in contact with a variety of short, musical calls. Scold call is a metallic and harsh *cheerrrrrr-rrr-rrr.*

habitat

Brushy thickets and ravines, woodland edges, brushy backyards, and gardens. Regularly nests near humans in garages, sheds, hanging baskets, old cans, etc.

backyard

Visits bird feeders for seed, suet, peanuts, and peanut butter. Also visits birdbaths. Will use nest boxes and any other small enclosed cavity for nesting, especially inside open buildings.

EASTERN BLUEBIRD

SIALIA SIALIS
SIZE: 7″

Bluebirds have a near-mythical status among North Americans because of their beauty, their sweetly musical song, and their willingness to use human-supplied housing. This beloved member of the thrush family has greatly benefited from the efforts of bluebird enthusiasts to provide safe and available nest boxes.

field marks

The adult male has a bright blue back, rusty breast, and white belly. The adult female is slightly paler overall. The juvenile is grayish, spotted with white. When perched, bluebirds have a hunch-backed appearance.

sounds

Song is a soft rich warble in short phrases: *tur, tur, turley, turley!* Flight call is a two-noted *ju-lee!* Warning call is a down-slurred *tyew!*

habitat

Open grassy habitat, including pastures, grassland, parks, roadsides. Bluebirds are still-hunters—they perch and watch for insects to move below them. They are often seen perching on fences, power lines, and exposed treetops.

backyard

If your backyard is open and grassy, the best way to attract bluebirds is to offer them nest boxes. They will also visit water features to drink and bathe. At feeders they are attracted to suet dough, suet, mealworms, peanut hearts, peanut butter, and fruit bits.

MOUNTAIN BLUEBIRD

SIALIA CURRUCOIDES
SIZE: 7¼"

Our all-blue bluebird, the mountain bluebird nests in open country at elevations above 5,000 feet in the West. This species often hovers while hunting for insect prey.

field marks

The male is sky blue above and light blue below. The female is light blue-gray overall, with darker blue wings. This bluebird is larger and longer-bodied than the western and eastern bluebirds, both of which show some rusty orange in their plumage.

sounds

Song is a soft warbled two-note phrase: *choo-lee.* Call is a thin, descending *wheew!*

habitat

Mountain bluebirds nest in open country. They winter in open lowlands with scattered trees. Found in flocks in winter.

backyard

Uses nest boxes in appropriate open habitat. Winter flocks may visit feeding stations for suet, suet dough, fruit bits, and mealworms and for water at birdbaths.

HYLOCICHLA
MUSTELINA
SIZE: 7¾"

WOOD THRUSH

This summer resident of eastern forests has a beautiful song that has enthralled many a poet-naturalist. Wood thrushes only rarely venture out of the deep woods, but their voice carries well beyond their preferred habitat.

field marks

This thrush is bright rusty brown on the head, back, and tail with a bright white chest and belly boldly patterned with large dark brown spots. No other thrush has such bold breast markings.

sounds

Song is a flutelike *ee-oh-lay* and similar phrases. Call is *tut-tut-tut*.

habitat

Cool and wet deciduous woods in spring and summer. Winters in the Neotropics.

backyard

If your backyard is in the East and is wooded or has old forest nearby, you will hear wood thrushes singing on summer mornings and evenings. They occasionally forage on wooded edges and may visit water features to drink and bathe.

AMERICAN ROBIN

TURDUS MIGRATORIUS
SIZE: 10″

You don't have to be a bird watcher to know the American robin. Its brick red breast and dark back are a familiar sight on lawns all across North America. Despite its reputation as a harbinger of spring, many robins spend the winter at northern latitudes, leaving open fields and lawns for the deep woods.

field marks

Males are darker backed than females. Young robins leave the nest before they can fly. They are spot-breasted with a bold white eye-ring.

sounds

Song is a rich warble: *cherrio-churry-lee, cheery-up, churr-lee*. During spring and summer, robins are often the first birds to sing in the morning and the last at night. Alarmed birds give a loud *seee!* The common call is *tut-tut-tut*.

habitat

Any kind of open ground is suitable for robins, which prefer to forage for earthworms when they're available. Lawns, parks, open meadows, and muddy fields are all likely places to find robins. When snow and ice cover the ground, robins take to the woods to forage for fruits and berries.

backyard

Robins will visit feeders for fruit, but you're more likely to see them on your lawn, where they'll find grubs and earthworms. For this reason, robins are often the unfortunate victims of chemically treated lawns. They also visit birdbaths.

GRAY CATBIRD

DUMETELLA CAROLINENSIS
SIZE: 8¾"

For a bird that mews like a cat and is gray overall, the gray catbird is well named. This common and widespread bird prefers thickets and is often seen before it is heard.

field marks

Only the dark cap and tail and chestnut undertail break up the catbird's overall gray coloration. Its bill, eyes, and legs are dark too.

sounds

Call is a catlike *meww!* Song is a jumble of phrases, some sweet, some nasal, without any regular repetition. Other common mimics (brown thrasher, northern mockingbird) repeat phrases in their songs.

habitat

Thick tangles and underbrush, also woodland edges.

backyard

Catbirds will forage and nest in dense hedgerows and shrubs. They visit backyards for fruiting trees and plants and for water at birdbaths. They occasionally take fruit bits and suet dough from feeders.

NORTHERN MOCKINGBIRD

Our most prolific mimic and singer, the northern mockingbird makes itself conspicuous with its loud and varied song, territorial ways, and the flashes of white in its wings and tail when it flies. It regularly attacks other birds and humans, as well as cats and other predators that cross its territory. It also defends its winter food sources.

field marks

The mockingbird is drab gray overall, darker on its back, with obvious white wing patches and outer tail feathers. It is longer billed, lighter colored, and more horizontal in perching posture than the similar loggerhead shrike.

sounds

Imitates other birds, whistles, telephones, barking dogs, and many other sounds in a series, with each phrase repeated more than two times. Young unmated males will sing at night in spring and summer. Call is a harsh *chak!* or a nasal *shairrr!*

habitat

Mockingbirds are often found near human habitation, including parks, gardens, farmyards, and brushy thickets along roadways. Ornamental fruit and berry-bearing trees and shrubs are often the center of a wintering mockingbird's territory.

backyard

Mockers will visit feeders for fruit, mealworms, suet, and suet dough. They may be bullies, chasing off other feeder visitors.

BOMBYCILLA CEDRORUM
SIZE: 7¼"

CEDAR WAXWING

This is the smaller, more widespread of our two waxwing species. Cedar waxwings are most often found in flocks, which roam far and wide seeking fruit-bearing trees.

field marks

The cedar waxwing is warm brown overall with a black mask, a crest (which may be raised or lowered), a bright yellow tail tip, and red waxy tips on its wings (for which the species is named). Juveniles are streaky overall. The larger Bohemian waxwing has a burnt orange undertail and more white in the wings.

sounds

Call is a high, reedy *tseeee*. Flocks give this call almost constantly.

habitat

In spring and summer, open forests, parks, orchards, and in trees near water over which the birds hawk insects. In winter, fruit-bearing trees and shrubs, including ornamental plantings in residential areas.

backyard

Will visit fruiting trees or shrubs in any season. Also attracted to water features and birdbaths. Does not typically visit feeders.

red   white-winged

LOXIA
CURVIROSTRA (left)
SIZE: 5¾"–7"

LOXIA
LEUCOPTERA (right)
SIZE: 6½"

RED CROSSBILL
WHITE-WINGED CROSSBILL

These two similar species share the oddly crossed mandibles for which they are named. These bills are perfect for prying seeds out of pine cones and the seed enclosures of other trees.

red

white-winged

field marks

Crossbills are large chunky finches with heavy, crossed mandibles. Males of both species are red overall, but coloration varies in intensity among individuals. Females are yellow to yellow-green. White-winged crossbills are slightly larger and show obvious white wing bars.

sounds

Red: song is a musical series of warbles and metallic clicks. Call is *jip-jip*. White-winged: song is a series of trills with loud chip notes interspersed. Call is *chit-chit-chit*.

habitat

Crossbills breed and forage in coniferous forests, especially spruce, hemlock, larch, and tamarack. In winter they may range far and wide in search of food.

backyard

Foraging flocks may visit feeders well to the south of the normal wintering range. They eat sunflower seed but are more likely to visit nearby stands of large cone-bearing conifers and to drink at water features.

eastern

spotted

SPOTTED TOWHEE
EASTERN TOWHEE

Our two bright orange, black, and white towhees were once considered a single species: the rufous-sided towhee. Now the dark-backed eastern birds are called eastern towhee, and the white-spotted-backed western birds are called spotted towhee.

spotted

eastern

field marks

Males of both species have a bold black head, red eyes, a rufous belly, and a long black tail edged in white. Females are browner. The dark back of the spotted towhee is covered in white spots. Both species are ground-loving birds that make their living scratching through the leaf litter for food.

sounds

Eastern towhee song: *drink-your-teeeeee!* Call: *chew-ink!*
Spotted towhee song: *Cheeeeeeee!* Call: a nasal *cheweee!*

habitat

Open woods, brushy areas, woodland edges, hedgerows, gardens, and bird feeders.

backyard

Both towhee species will visit feeders for seed scattered on the ground, especially mixed seed, cracked corn, and millet. They will also visit birdbaths to drink and bathe.

SPIZELLA PASSERINA
SIZE: 5½"

CHIPPING SPARROW

Often overlooked because of its nonmusical song and small size, the "chippie" is one of our most common sparrows.

field marks

Slender and flat-headed, with a plain gray breast and a long tail, the male has an obvious rusty cap in breeding plumage. In fall (nonbreeding plumage), adults appear streaky-capped with a dull gray eye line. Several similar-looking (and closely related) sparrows also visit backyards and feeding stations, including the tree sparrow, field sparrow, and clay-colored sparrow.

sounds

Song is a long, dry trill on a single pitch. Call is a thin *seet*.

habitat

Young woodlands and woodland edges, pines, farms, orchards, gardens, and landscaped suburban backyards.

backyard

A common feeder visitor, except when insects are abundantly available. Prefers mixed seed and cracked corn scattered on the ground or in low platform feeders. Visits water features and often nests in low shrubbery in gardens, parks, and backyards.

SONG SPARROW

MELOSPIZA MELODIA
SIZE: 6¼»

A common backyard bird across most of North America, the song sparrow is equally happy living in a suburban backyard or along the edge of a remote forest. It is named for its pleasing song, which it sings regularly throughout the spring, summer, and fall.

field marks

The song sparrow is medium sized with a long round-tipped tail and a heavily streaked breast with a central breast spot. This species varies quite a bit in color and size, from the pale eastern birds to the darker western birds.

sounds

Song is a series of musical notes with a few buzzy tones interspersed. It typically starts with three or four clear notes: *sweet-sweet-sweet* . . .

habitat

Brushy habitat, thickets, woodland edges, old meadows, gardens, parks, and shrubbery.

backyard

Song sparrows will scratch for seed bits below your bird feeder. They will also eat sunflower bits, peanut bits, and suet dough from a low platform feeder. They visit water features to drink and bathe.

baltimore   bullock's

ICTERUS
GALBULA (left)
SIZE: 8½"

ICTERUS
BULLOCKII (right)
SIZE: 8½"

BALTIMORE ORIOLE
BULLOCK'S ORIOLE

These are bright orange and black birds with a slender bill. The range of each species covers about half of North America: Baltimore in the East and Bullock's in the West.

baltimore

bullock's

field marks

Males of both species are deep orange. Females have a light gray-buffy body and pale orange head. The male Baltimore has an all-black hood. The male Bullock's has a black cap and throat offset by orange cheeks and large white wing patches on black wings.

sounds

Baltimore: a treetop singer. Beautiful whistled notes in a series: *See me? Here I am! Up here!* He also sings a series of chattery notes.
Bullock's: paired notes in a series. Also a hoarse chatter.

habitat

Baltimore: open deciduous woods, parks, and backyards with large shade trees.
Bullock's: riparian woods, shade trees in parks and farmyards, woodlots.

backyard

Both species will visit feeders for orange or grapefruit halves and occasionally for suet or suet dough. They're also attracted to nectar at hummingbird feeders and grape jelly at oriole feeders. They will visit birdbaths to bathe and drink.

PIRANGA
OLIVACEA
SIZE: 7"

SCARLET TANAGER

The breeding-plumage adult male scarlet tanager is hard to confuse with any other species, but in fall he loses his scarlet plumage, retaining only the black wings and tail. This treetop singer is often heard before it is seen, despite its brilliant coloration.

field marks

The breeding male is bright red with black wings and tail and a pale bill. Females and nonbreeding males are yellow-green overall, but males have darker wings. Similar species include the all-red summer tanager of the South and Southwest and the western tanager, which has a red head and yellow body.

sounds

Song sounds like a sore-throated American robin: *churry-cheery-churry-cheery*. Call is a *chip-burr*.

habitat

Mixed woodlands, especially oaks, large shade trees, and forested parks.

backyard

Scarlet tanagers might be most attracted to birdbaths, especially if they have moving water. They will also visit feeders for fruit, suet dough, and mealworms, but this is uncommon.

PIRANGA
LUDOVICIANA
SIZE: 7¼"

WESTERN TANAGER

The strikingly marked male western tanager is hard to confuse with any other bird. This species spends summers in the coniferous forests of the West and winters in the Neotropics.

field marks

Both sexes show bold yellow and white wing bars, a key field mark for this species (no other tanager has wing bars). Breeding adult males have a bright orange-red head and a boldly contrasting yellow and black body, wings, and tail. Fall and winter males are yellow overall with black wings and tail. Some retain a little red on the face. A stout, pale bill helps separate this tanager from orioles.

sounds

Song consists of short, hoarse phrases similar to those of the American robin but less musical. Call is a distinctive *pre-tee-tee!*

habitat

Conifer-covered mountains and mixed forests in summer, other wooded habitats in migration.

backyard

The western tanager may pass through your yard in migration, foraging high in the trees. It may visit feeders for fruit bits or take nectar at hummingbird feeders. It may also visit water features to drink or bathe.

CARDINALIS CARDINALIS
SIZE: 8¾"

NORTHERN CARDINAL

The male cardinal is hard to mistake for any other species. It is our only all-red bird with a prominent crest. It's a common year-round resident of the eastern United States and southernmost Canada, as well as the desert Southwest to Arizona.

field marks

Adult males are bright red with a red crest, black face, and orange-pink bill. Adult females are rosy brown overall with a red-tipped crest, black face, and pale pink bill. Juveniles are all brown with a dark gray bill.

sounds

Song is loud and variable series of whistled notes: *sweet-CHEER CHEER CHEER!* Or *purty-purty-purty.* Call is a loud, metallic *teek!*

habitat

Open woods, woodland edges, farmyards, parks, and backyards and gardens with thick brush.

backyard

Readily visits feeders for sunflower seeds, peanuts, suet dough, and mealworms. Also visits water features to bathe and drink.

ROSE-BREASTED GROSBEAK

PHEUCTICUS LUDOVICIANUS

SIZE: 8"

A medium-sized songbird with a large seed-crushing bill, the rose-breasted grosbeak spends the breeding season in deciduous woods across the northern portions of North America. It winters in the Neotropics.

field marks

Adult males in breeding plumage show an obvious rose-colored V on the breast. The head, back, wings, and tail are mostly black. The wing bars, flanks, and rump are bright white. Females and young birds are streaked with brown, like an oversized female purple finch.

sounds

Song is a series of rich, warbled phrases, similar to that of the American robin. Call is *eek!*, like a tennis shoe squeaking on a gym floor. This note is often the first clue to this species' presence.

habitat

Deciduous woods, parks, and orchards. Visits feeders in spring and summer.

backyard

Grosbeaks eat black-oil and striped sunflower seeds at feeders. They also visit water features to drink and bathe.

BLACK-HEADED GROSBEAK

PHEUCTICUS MELANO-CEPHALUS
SIZE: 8¼"

As its name suggests, the chunky-looking black-headed grosbeak has a big powerful bill perfectly designed for cracking seeds. Breeding-plumaged males are boldly marked with orange, black, and white.

field marks

Adult males in breeding plumage have a black head, orange body, black tail, and black wings with bold white wing bars. Females and immatures show a buffy breast and streaky back. Flying birds show yellow wing linings. Males in nonbreeding plumage lack the all-black head.

sounds

Song is a series of musical phrases, rising and falling—similar to the song of the American robin. Call is a loud, sharp *eek!*

habitat

Woodlands and woodland edges.

backyard

Visits backyard feeding stations for all types of sunflower seed.

PLANTING FOR HUMMINGBIRDS

chapter three

Everything about hummingbirds is magical. Nearly every gardener knows that hummingbirds zip from flower to flower to sip nectar. They can miraculously hover in midair, insert their bills deep into a bloom, then back up and probe another flower in the cluster before speeding off. These diminutive, jewel-like creatures never cease to amaze.

Despite their small size (ruby-throated hummingbirds are only 3 to 3¾ inches long; calliope hummingbirds between 2¾ and 3½ inches), they are spectacular fliers that can make swift, aerial starts and stops like no other bird. Hummingbirds can fly forward at speeds clocked as fast as 50 to 60 miles per hour. In addition to hovering in place, they can also fly straight up, straight down, and backward.

Most hummingbirds migrate over long distances. Ruby-throated hummingbirds, the only species that nests east of the Mississippi River, winters from southern Texas to Costa Rica in Central America. In summer, it ranges as far north as southern Canada. Rufous hummingbirds winter in Mexico and

Western states are rich in both hummingbirds and hummingbird plants. This desert scene features ocotillo (*Fouquieria splendens*), which produces scarlet, orange-red, or creamy yellow flowers that attract hummingbirds as well as orioles.

summer as far north as southern Alaska and the Yukon Territory. Western species frequently migrate up the Sierra and Rocky Mountains as spring arrives and flowers open.

While gardeners in the eastern states see only ruby-throated hummingbirds, western gardeners routinely see eight or more species. Black-chinned, calliope, broad-tailed, and rufous hummingbirds are widely distributed in the West. (Black-chinned, calliope, ruby-throated, and rufous hummingbirds nest into Canada.) In addition to some of these species, California gardeners also can see Anna's, Costa's, and Allen's hummingbirds. Twenty-one species enter the United States, but most don't penetrate far beyond the Mexican border. Southern Arizona and the Big Bend area in Texas are the best places to see these rarer migrants.

HUMMINGBIRD FEEDERS

Hummingbird feeders offer an ideal way to attract these jewels of the air, and a good way to supplement the flower nectar your garden supplies. Several styles of feeders are available commercially, or you can make your own by putting red nail polish or a red ribbon on the type of water bottle used for pet hamsters and gerbils. Hang your feeder in view of a window so you can enjoy the show.

You can buy packets of nectar mix or make your own using one part ordinary white sugar and four parts water. Boil the mixture and let it cool before filling and hanging the feeder. Store leftover mixture in the refrigerator. It isn't necessary to add red food coloring. Never use honey instead of sugar; it has been shown to support bacterial growth that can be fatal to hummingbirds.

Empty the feeder and change the solution every 2 to 3 days (every 2 days if temperatures are above 60°F) to avoid offering nectar mixture that has been contaminated by bacteria. Always wash out the feeder thoroughly with scalding water before refilling.

what attracts hummingbirds?

A WELL-DESIGNED BIRD GARDEN will also attract hummingbirds. Like songbirds, humming-birds need food, water, cover, and nest sites. Flower nectar provides an important part of every hummingbird's diet. Tubular or trumpet-shaped blooms that are bright red or orange in color attract them like magnets. Although a hummingbird's slender, pointed bill is designed specifically for feeding from tubular flowers, they also visit many other kinds of flowers, from white and lilac hosta flowers to zinnias, begonias, and sweet William.

Hummingbirds have such fast metabolism that they must feed almost con-stantly during daylight hours. (A hummingbird's tongue has either a tubular or brushlike tip; to sip nectar, it opens its beak slightly and laps the nectar with the tip of the tongue.) They store food in their crops to sustain them overnight. In cool weather or during cold spring nights, they can tempo-rarily enter a state of dormancy, called torpor, to conserve food reserves. Torpid birds have lowered body temperatures, heart rates, and breathing rates.

Use the lists in this chapter to identify plants that will attract humming-birds to your garden. Plan for a constant supply of blooms from late spring or early summer to late summer or early fall, depending on when hum-mingbirds are in your area. (Wild bird centers or birding clubs can tell you when they should be in your area; gardeners in the warmest parts of the Southwest can have hummingbirds year-round.) You can add annuals and perennials that attract them into any of your beds and borders, or plant a garden that features only hummingbird flowers. Add shrubs and vines that attract hummingbirds to shrub borders and foundation plantings. Vines are especially effective when trained on a trellis near a window so you can watch the birds feeding, but a freestanding arbor or a trellis behind flower beds is also effective. Vines can also be trained up fences and trees and allowed to spill over shrubs.

Orioles feed on many plants that attract hummingbirds, including trumpet vines (*Campsis radicans*), honeysuckle (*Lonicera* spp.), and daylilies. They also visit hummingbird feeders for nectar. Special oriole feeders are available; they are orange in color and somewhat larger than hummingbird feeders. Orioles prefer a slightly more diluted sugar mixture. Boil one part sugar in six parts water. Replace the mixture and clean the feeder every 2 to 3 days, just as you would for hummingbirds.

Hummingbirds guard feeding and nesting territories during the breeding season, so try to scatter plants that attract them throughout your yard. (Males guard feeding territories and use them to attract females. The females, which build the nests and raise the young alone, establish nesting territories and drive away other hummingbirds.) Or plant two hummingbird gardens, one in the backyard and another in the front, out of sight of the first.

In addition to nectar, some species also eat flower pollen and tree sap. Hummingbirds have been observed feeding on sap running from tree wounds, as well as from the holes drilled by sapsuckers.

Insects are an important part of every hummingbird's diet. They eat a wide variety of them, including aphids, gnats, mosquitoes, flying ants, leafhoppers, and flies, as well as small beetles, bugs, and weevils. Beneficial spiders and parasitic wasps are also common fare. Hummingbirds frequently catch insects and spiders on the flowers they frequent in their search for nectar. Daddy longlegs, or harvestmen, are another common prey. Ruby-throated hummingbirds have been observed picking insects out of spider webs.

Bee balm (*Monarda didyma*) is a member of the mint family, with fragrant leaves and clusters of red flowers. It spreads quickly by underground runners, so grow it in wild areas or plant it in bottomless buckets sunk in the soil to contain its spreading.

Hummingbirds build their diminutive nests from a variety of materials, such as milkweed or thistledown, held together by spider webs. The outsides of the nests are often decorated with bits of lichen and moss.

OTHER HUMMINGBIRD GARDEN FEATURES

A yard that offers a mix of sun and shade is ideal for attracting hummingbirds. Many of the flowers they feed from grow best in sunny beds, borders, or meadow plantings. Wooded areas provide ideal nest sites. Hummingbirds construct their tiny, cup-shaped nests from a variety of materials that are fastened together with spider webs. (An organic garden that is rich in spiders will ensure a ready supply for your visitors.) The sites selected vary by species, but areas of open or dense woods or forest margins, sometimes over a stream, are common. They construct nests from such materials as milkweed or thistledown, soft ferns, moss, and grasses. Several species decorate the outside of the nest with lichen until it blends in with the branch to which it is attached.

To make a birdbath or other water feature especially appealing to hummingbirds, consider adding a device that produces a fine spray or mist above it. (These are available from wild bird centers.) Hummingbirds are designed for a life in the air and will actually bathe by repeatedly flying through the mist. They will also alight on a twig positioned near water.

flowers for hummingbirds

BECAUSE MANY ANNUALS BLOOM FROM SPRING OR EARLY SUMMER THROUGH FROST, they provide a steady supply of nectar for hummingbirds all season long. Mix these reliable, easy-to-grow plants into beds and borders along with perennials to create a showy display that both you and the hummingbirds will adore. Or grow a bed of annuals alone that changes design every year. You can also edge shrub borders or foundation plantings with annuals, or plant them in the herb or vegetable garden. Gardeners in southern zones—in the South, Southwest, and lower elevations of California—will find a number of tender perennials that are grown as annuals in the North but can be grown as perennials in the South.

HOLLYHOCKS

The tall spikes of hollyhocks appeal to hummingbirds and gardeners alike. Look for single-flowered types, which have showy summer blooms in burgundy, red, deep pink, orange-yellow, and white. Although they are officially biennials, hollyhocks are short-lived perennials in the right conditions. They also reseed.

ALCEA ROSEA

ZONES:
2–9

culture

Plant hollyhocks in deep, rich, well-drained soil in full sun. A site out of the wind is important; otherwise these tall plants need staking. Sow seeds indoors in winter for bloom the following summer, or sow outdoors in summer for bloom the following summer.

Hollyhocks (*Alcea rosea*).

SNAPDRAGONS

Snapdragons are perennials grown as half-hardy annuals. These erect or spreading plants bear spikes of red, burgundy, orange, pink, yellow, and white blooms. Their early spring blooms provide nectar when hummingbird flowers can be scarce. Plants range from dwarfs under 1 foot to 3-foot plants that require staking.

ANTIRRHINUM MAJUS

ZONES:
7–10

culture

Snapdragons prefer cool temperatures and will even survive light frost. Plant them outdoors in full sun and rich, well-drained soil as soon as the soil can be worked in spring. Remove spent blooms to prolong flowering. Sow seeds outdoors in a shaded spot in late summer for a fall crop of blooms.

Snapdragons (*Antirrhinum majus*) are easy-to-grow annuals with spikes of brightly colored blooms that attract hummingbirds.

COLUMBINES

Columbines provide an important source of nectar for hummingbirds in spring and early summer. The blue-green compound foliage is delicate looking and attractive. Wild columbine (*Aquilegia canadensis*) bears dangling red-and-yellow flowers on 1- to 3-foot plants; crimson columbine (*A. formosa*) resembles it, but is native to the western United States. Hybrid columbines with red and pink flowers are also good choices.

AQUILEGIA SPP.

ZONES:
4–9

culture

Grow columbines in full sun to partial shade. Moist, well-drained, sandy to loamy soil is ideal.

CANNAS

Cannas are tuberous-rooted tender perennials that are grown as annuals in northern zones. They feature bold, tropical-looking leaves and clusters of showy red, orange, or yellow summer flowers. Height can range from 3 to 6 feet or more. Cannas generally look best planted in a bed by themselves or among tall, bold perennials, large annuals, and ornamental grasses.

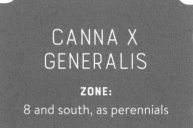

CANNA X GENERALIS

ZONE:
8 and south, as perennials

culture

Rich, well-drained, evenly moist soil and a site in full sun is essential. Plant outdoors in spring when soil temperatures reach 65°F—about the time tomatoes can be planted. Roots can be dug in fall and overwintered indoors like dahlias.

FOXGLOVES

Foxgloves bear erect spikes of tubular flowers in deep pink, rose, white, or yellow atop rosettes of large, broad, lance-shaped leaves. Common foxglove *(Digitalis purpurea)* is a biennial or short-lived perennial that ranges from 2 to 5 feet. Strawberry foxglove *(D. x mertonensis)* bears rose-pink flowers and is a short-lived perennial. It is 3 to 4 feet tall.

DIGITALIS SPP.

ZONES:
3–8, depending on
the species

culture

Grow foxgloves in full sun or partial shade in evenly moist, well-drained soil that is rich in organic matter. Both species will self-sow. Divide *D. x mertonensis* every 2 to 3 years to maintain its perennial character.

Foxglove *(Digitalis purpurea)* produces spikes of trumpet-shaped, rosy purple, pink, or white flowers in spring and early summer.

DAYLILIES

Daylilies produce trumpet-shaped flowers, each of which lasts only a day, above clumps of strap-shaped leaves in summer. Plants range from 2 to over 4 feet in height. Hummingbirds visit lemon daylily *(Hemerocallis lilio-asphodelus)* and tawny daylily *(H. fulva)*, as well as hybrids with vivid red, orange, pink, and yellow flowers.

HEMEROCALLIS SPP.

ZONES:
2–9, depending on the species

culture

Grow daylilies in full sun in average to rich soil that is moist but well drained. They will also tolerate light shade.

Hummingbirds will visit daylilies with yellow or orange flowers, but they are particularly attracted to red-hued cultivars, including 'Pardon Me', 'Christmas Carol', 'Royal Mountie', 'Scarlet Apache', and 'Red Monarch' (shown here).

HIBISCUS, ROSE MALLOW

These tropical-looking plants bear large red, rose, pink, or white saucer-shaped flowers atop 5- to 8-foot plants. The leaves are broad and maplelike. Both scarlet rose mallow *(Hibiscus coccineus)* and rose mallow *(H. moscheutos)* are good choices.

HIBISCUS SPP.

ZONES:
5–10, depending
on the species

culture

Grow hibiscus in moist, well-drained soil that is rich in organic matter. They will grow in full sun or partial shade.

Common rose mallow *(Hibiscus moscheutos)* is a hardy perennial that bears its dramatic pink, red, or white flowers all summer long. 'Lord Baltimore' is shown here.

LILIES

The trumpet-, cup-, or bowl-shaped flowers of many lilies are ideal for attracting hummingbirds. These stately bulbs range from 2 to 8 feet or more in height and have narrow grasslike or lance-shaped leaves. Hummingbirds visit several native species of lilies that have red to orange-red or orange flowers, including Canada lily *(Lilium canadense)*, wood lily *(L. philadelphicum)*, Turk's-cap lily *(L. superbum)*, and tiger lily *(L. lancifolium)*. Hummingbirds would also appreciate the many hybrid lilies with bright flowers that are available.

LILIUM SPP.

ZONES:
3–9, depending on the species

culture

Lilies demand well-drained soil that is deep, rich, and loamy. The pH should be neutral to slightly acid, although some species tolerate alkaline soils. A site in full sun is best, but native lilies will tolerate partial shade.

Asiatic hybrid lilies, such as this 'Red Alert', bloom early in lily season, are easy to grow, and multiply quickly.

CARDINAL FLOWER

No hummingbird garden should be without a clump of this native wildflower, which bears spikes of scarlet flowers in late summer above clumps of lance-shaped leaves. Plants reach 2 to 4 feet. Cultivars with burgundy and ruby-red flowers are available.

LOBELIA CARDINALIS

ZONES:
2–9

culture

Cardinal flowers need constantly moist soil in partial to full shade. Plant them along streams or ponds, and even drainage ditches. Divide plants every 2 years; they can be short-lived, and division helps keep them vigorous.

BEE BALM, BERGAMOT, OSWEGO TEA

As its common name implies, bee balm is attractive to bees, but hummingbirds and butterflies also frequent its somewhat ragged-looking clusters of tube-shaped flowers. The leaves are fragrant and minty and the plants range from 2 to 4 feet. 'Marshall's Delight' is a pink-flowered, mildew-resistant cultivar. 'Gardenview Scarlet' bears large red flowers and is also mildew resistant.

MONARDA DIDYMA

ZONES:
4–8

culture

Grow bee balm in any good soil that remains evenly moist. The plants will grow in full sun or partial shade. Since they spread quickly, divide them frequently in spring. Or plant them in an out-of-the-way spot in a wild garden where they can spread unimpeded.

FLOWERING TOBACCO

Hummingbirds visit the fragrant trumpets of flowering tobaccos, which are tender perennials grown as annuals. *Nicotiana* x *sanderae* and its cultivars, including 'Crimson Rock', 'Breakthrough Mix', and 'Niki Series', are especially effective because they come in crimson-red, rose-pink, and white. *N. alata* and *N. sylvestris* also are effective; plants with white flowers are most common, but cultivars with red, pink, or purplish blooms are available. Plants range from 1 to 3 feet.

NICOTIANA SPP.

ZONES: 10–11

culture

Plant flowering tobacco in partial shade or full sun. Grow from seed sown in the garden after all danger of frost has past. Or start seedlings indoors 6 to 8 weeks before the last spring frost and move transplants to the garden 2 weeks after the last frost date. Do not cover the seed, as it requires light to germinate.

Flowering tobacco (*Nicotiana*).

PENSTEMONS, BEARDTONGUES

These spring- and summer-blooming perennials bear racemes of two-lipped tubular flowers in bright colors, including scarlet, purple, lavender-blue, yellow, or white, on plants that range from 3 or 4 inches to 6 feet or more. Most penstemons are native to western North America and can be difficult to grow outside their native habitats. Hybrid penstemons are among the best choices for eastern gardens, where summer heat and humidity are problematic. These include 'Firebird', 'Ruby', and 'Garnet', along with hairy beardtongue (*Penstemon hirsutus*). Other penstemons to try include common beardtongue (*P. barbatus*) and its cultivar 'Prairie Fire', *P. pinifolius*, and *P. smallii*.

PENSTEMON SPP.

ZONES:
3–8

culture

Penstemons require well-drained sandy or loamy soil that is rich in humus. Grow them in full sun or light shade. Divide plants every 4 to 5 years to keep them vigorous.

Ruby-throated Hummingbird (*Archilochus colubris*) male at Prairie Fire Penstemon (*Penstemon barbatus*) Shelby, Illinois, USA.

PETUNIAS

Petunias are sprawling, 8- to 18-inch plants that bear trumpet-shaped blooms in red, deep pink, purple, blue, and white. Many striped or barred types are available too, including red and pink blooms with stripes or white edges. For hummingbirds, avoid double flowers. Chose multiflora or milliflora types, which have smaller and more plentiful flowers and are more disease resistant than grandifloras.

PETUNIA X HYBRIDA

ZONES: 10–11

culture

Move transplants to the garden after danger of frost has passed. They prefer full sun, warm weather, and good, well-drained garden soil. Water frequently during hot weather. Shear plants back and feed them after the main flush of blooms to encourage them to produce additional flowers.

Hummingbirds will visit flowers such as these petunias. Planting them in window boxes will give you a front-row seat for easy viewing. Also consider planting tubs and containers on decks and patios with hummingbird-attracting plants.

PHLOX

Phlox bear tubular flowers with five petals and can range from ground-hugging 4-inch plants to stately 4-foot plants for the perennial border. The flowers can be lavender, purple, pink, red, or white. Hummingbirds will visit a variety of phlox species, regardless of their color, including wild blue phlox (*Phlox divaricata*), Douglas's phlox (*P. douglasii*), creeping phlox (*P. stolonifera*), Carolina phlox (*P. Carolina*), moss pink (*P. subulata*), garden phlox (*P. paniculata*), and wild sweet William (*P. maculata*). Red-flowered selections hummingbirds especially enjoy include *P. paniculata* 'Starfire', *P. douglasii* 'Cracker Jack', and *P. subulata* 'Scarlet Flame'.

PHLOX SPP.

ZONES:
2–9, depending on the species

culture

Grow woodland natives *P. divaricata* and *P. stolonifera* in partial to full shade in rich, evenly moist soil. Grow the other species in full sun or very light shade. *P. douglasii* and *P. subulata* will grow in sandy or loamy soil that is well drained. The others require rich soil that is evenly moist but well drained.

Early-blooming flowers such as this creeping phlox (*Phlox subulata*) provide an important source of nectar for hummingbirds in spring. 'Candy Stripe' is shown here.

SAGES

Hummingbirds visit several members of this genus. Scarlet sage *(Salvia splendens)*, probably the most common, bears erect spikes of flaming red flowers on 1- to 3-foot plants. Texas sage *(S. coccinea)* bears its red blooms on 1- to 2-foot plants. Both are tender perennials grown as annuals in the North. Pineapple sage *(S. elegans)* flowers in the fall on 3- to 4-foot plants and is a perennial in Zone 9 and south. Autumn sage *(S. gregii)* is a Texas native with red to purplish red flowers that is hardy in Zone 7 and south. Both are grown as annuals in the North.

SALVIA SPP.

ZONES:
6–11, depending on the species

culture

Plant salvias outdoors in full sun after all danger of frost has passed. Give plenty of water in dry weather. In the South, Southwest, and lower elevations of California, plants benefit from light to moderate shade. Take cuttings of perennial salvias in fall and root and overwinter them indoors.

Sages (*Salvia* spp.) bear flowers all summer long. Edging a bed with a block of these blooms or mixing them in with annuals or perennials is a surefire way to roll out the welcome mat for hummingbirds, such as this ruby-throat.

GARDEN NASTURTIUM

Nasturtiums are annuals that bear round leaves and showy red, orange, or yellow trumpetlike flowers all summer long. Both low-growing and climbing plants are available. Climbing nasturtiums require a trellis and can reach 10 feet in height. In addition to visiting the flowers for nectar, hummingbirds also undoubtedly feast on the aphids that commonly attack nasturtiums.

TROPAEOLUM MAJUS

ZONES: 2–11, depending on the species

culture

Grow nasturtiums in average to poor, well-drained soil; rich soil encourages lush foliage at the expense of flowers. Sow seed outside 2 weeks before the last spring frost. Nasturtiums transplant with difficulty but can be grown indoors in peat pots and moved after the last spring frost. These plants prefer cool temperatures and will not grow well in the Southeast during the hot summer months.

Nasturtium floridanum

GARDEN VERBENA

Verbenas bear rounded clusters of small fragrant flowers in red, pink, purple, yellow, and white from summer to fall. The plants can be trailing or upright, but are generally under 1 foot in height. Common garden verbena *(Verbena x hybrida)*, a tender perennial grown as an annual, comes in a variety of colors, including vivid scarlet. *V. peruviana* bears red flowers and is hardy in Zone 9 and south, but is commonly grown as an annual in the North. *V.* 'Taylortown Red' and *V.* 'Flame' have vivid scarlet flowers and are hardy in Zones 6–9.

VERBENA SPP.

ZONES: 3–11, depending on the species

culture

Grow verbenas in full sun, except in the Deep South and desert areas, where light shade is best to reduce drought stress. Transplant after all danger of frost has past. Deadhead flowers to keep new blooms coming. In areas where they cannot be grown as perennials, take cuttings in fall and root and overwinter them indoors.

Verbena x hybrida

MORE FLOWERS FOR HUMMINGBIRDS

Once blazing red flowers lure humming-birds to your garden, they're likely to sip from a variety of blooms. Here are some more flowers you can add to your plantings.

PERENNIALS

Buddleia spp. Butterfly bushes

Castileja spp. Paintbrushes

Crocosmia spp. Montbretia, *crocosmia*, including *C. masoniorum* and its cultivar 'Firebird', *C.* x *crocosmiiflora* 'Emily McKenzie', and hybrids such as 'Lucifer' and 'Emberglow'

Delphinium spp. Delphiniums, especially *D. cardinale* and *D. nudicale*

Dianthus spp. Pinks, carnations, including *D.* x *allwoodii*, *D. deltoides*, and *D. plumarius*

Epilobium angustifolium Fireweed

Gentiana septemfida var. *lagodechiana* Crested gentian

Heuchera sanguinea Coralbells

Hosta spp. Hostas, funkia, plantain lilies

Kniphofia uvuaria Red-hot poker

Liatris spp. Gayfeathers, blazing stars

Lycoris spp. Spider lilies, magic lilies, especially *L. radiata* and *L. squamigera*

Saponaria officinalis Bouncing bet

Scabiosa caucasica Pincushion flower

Silene spp. Catchfly, campion, including *S. virginica* and *S. regia*

Yucca spp. Yucca, Adam's needle

Coralbells (*Heuchera sanguinea*)

Butterfly bush (*Buddleia davidii*)

Red-hot poker (*Kniphofia uvaria* 'Flamenco')

Pincushion flower
(*Scabiosa caucasica*)

ANNUALS

Begonia x *Semperflorens-cultorum* hybrids.
Wax begonias
Cleome hasslerana Spider flower, cleome
Consolida spp. Larkspur
Dahlia hybrids Dahlias
Dianthus barbatus Sweet William
Gladiolus spp. Gladiolus, including
G. *communis*, hardy in Zones 6–10,
and G. x *hortulanus*, hardy in Zones
7–10, but grown as an annual in
the North

Miriabilis jalapa Four-o'clocks, marvel
of Peru
Pelargonium spp. Zonal geraniums
Scabiosa atropurpurea Pincushion flower
Tagetes spp. Marigolds
Tithonia rotundifolia Mexican sunflower
Zinnia spp. Zinnias

Spider flower (*Cleome hasslerana*)

Gladiolus 'Far West'

Four-o'clocks
(*Mirabilis jalapa*)

vines for hummingbirds

VINES ARE STUNNING TRAINED OVER A TRELLIS NEAR A PATIO OR ON A DECK, or at the back of a flower garden. They also have a nice effect covering a fence.

TRUMPET VINE

The orange to orange-red blooms of trumpet vine are classic hummingbird plants. *Campsis radicans* bears an abundance of orange, orange-red, or yellow 3-inch-long trumpets in summer and early fall. 'Crimson Trumpet' has red flowers without orange overtones. *C. x tagliabuana* 'Mme. Galen' bears rich orange-pink trumpets. Both are woody vines that climb to between 30 and 40 feet and bear compound leaves.

CAMPSIS

ZONES:
5–9

culture

Trumpet vines are easy to grow in any soil and can be rampant in rich soil. Full sun is best, but plants will tolerate light shade. Prune the plants in spring to keep them in bounds and to keep them from becoming top-heavy. Top-heavy plants can pull away from their support.

Trumpet vine (*Campsis radicans*) is a vigorous climber that produces its red-orange trumpets in summer and early fall.

IPOMOEAS, MORNING GLORIES

Hummingbirds adore several of the easy-to-grow annual vines in this genus, which bear their blooms from early summer to fall. Cardinal climber (*Ipomoea multifida*) bears crimson trumpets with white eyes and has triangular-oval leaves. Cypress vine (*I. quamoclit*) also bears red trumpet-shaped flowers but has fernlike leaves. Red morning glory (*I. coccinea*) has fragrant red flowers and heart-shaped leaves. All generally climb to between 10 and 12 feet in an average summer; they can reach 25 feet or more in southern climates, where the growing season is long.

IPOMOEA

ZONES: 2–11, depending on the species

culture

Grow ipomoeas in well-drained, average soil in a warm, sunny location, and keep the plants well watered. For best results, nick the hard seed coats with a nail file, or soak them for 8 hours in tepid water before sowing. Although the seeds can be sown outdoors after all danger of frost has passed, it's best to start them indoors 6 to 8 weeks before the last frost. Sow seeds in peat pots, and transplant the seedlings with care, as they resent being disturbed.

Cypress vine (*Ipomoea quamoclit*).

HONEYSUCKLE

Both scarlet trumpet honeysuckle (*Lonicera* x *brownii*) and trumpet honeysuckle (*L. sempervirens*) make good additions to a hummingbird garden. Both bear clusters of narrow, red-to-orange trumpets in spring or early summer on twining, woody stems with oval leaves. Plants range from 12 to 20 feet in height. *L.* x *brownii* 'Dropmore Scarlet' has vivid red flowers that appear from early summer to fall.

LONICERA SPP.

ZONES:
4–9

culture

Grow honeysuckles in moist, well-drained soil that is slightly acid to near neutral. A site in full sun is best, but plants will tolerate light shade. Prune plants immediately after they flower to control the shape; be sure not to prune in late winter to early spring or you will remove most of the flower buds.

Trumpet honeysuckle (*Lonicera sempervirens*) is an easy-to-grow vine that bears clusters of narrow, trumpet-shaped blooms in spring.

SCARLET RUNNER BEANS

Scarlet runner beans are tender perennials commonly grown as annuals in vegetable gardens rather than flower beds. Hummingbirds don't care where they find the racemes of scarlet flowers. Plants have attractive blue-green leaves and will climb to 10 feet. The flowers are followed by tasty beans with somewhat fuzzy pods.

PHASEOLUS COCCINEUS

ZONES:
4–9

culture

Grow scarlet runner beans in rich, well-drained soil in full sun. Sow seeds outdoors after the last spring frost date.

Closeup of runner bean flower (*Phaseolus coccineus*).

trees and shrubs for hummingbirds

HUMMINGBIRDS VISIT THE FLOWERS OF MANY KINDS OF TREES AND SHRUBS. Consider including one or more of the following in your butterfly garden. Plants marked with a bird symbol 🐦 will also attract songbirds.

Abelia grandiflora Glossy abelia

Aesculus pavia Red buckeye

Albizia julibrissin Mimosa, silk tree

Caragana arborescens Siberian pea tree

Chaenomeles speciosa Common flowering quince

Crataegus phaenopyrum Washington hawthorn 🐦

Hibiscus syriacus Rose of Sharon, shrub althaea

Kolkwitzia amabilis Beautybush

Malus spp. Crab apples, apples

Rhododendron spp. Rhododendrons and azaleas

Robinia pseudoacacia Black locust

Syringa spp. Lilacs

Vitex agnus-castus Chaste tree

Weigela florida Old-fashioned weigela

Rose of Sharon (*Hibiscus syriacus* 'Aphrodite').

Common flowering quince (*Chaenomeles speciosa*).

Common lilacs *(Syringa vulgaris)* bear spring clusters of fragrant flowers in pale lilac, deep purple, pink, magenta, or white.

Chaste tree *(Vitex agnus-castus).*

hummingbird plants for southern zones

A WEALTH OF HUMMINGBIRD PLANTS exist for gardeners living in Zones 8, 9, 10, and 11. The following list includes some of the best plants to consider, but it is by no means complete. Many of the plants below come in a wide range of colors: when planting any hummingbird garden, take time to search out the brightest-colored cultivars you can find.

Many of these plants can be grown as pot plants that can summer outdoors and spend winter protected in a greenhouse or indoors. These include *Abutilon*, *Aloe*, *Fuchsia*, *Hibiscus*, and *Justicia*. In some cases, all they need to survive outdoors a zone north of where they are hardy is winter protection for a few crucial months when temperatures dip too low.

Agave spp.

Bottlebrush
(*Callistemon citrinus*).

Cigar plant or firecracker plant (*Cuphea micropetala*).

Fuchsia 'Swingtime'.

Abutilon spp. Flowering maple. Zones 9–11

Agave spp. Century plant, especially
A. americana. Zones 9–11

Aloe spp. Aloes, including *Aloe arborescens*,
A. aristata, A. brevifolia, A. ferox, A. humilis,
A. saponaria, and A. striata.
Zones 9–11

Caesalpinia gilliesii Bird-of-paradise shrub.
Zones 8–11

Callistemon spp. Bottlebrushes, including
C. citrinus, C. rigidus, and C. eriophylla.
Zones 8–11

Cercidium floridum Palo verde. Zones 9–11

Cestrum spp. Cestrums or jessamines,
including C. aurantiacum, C. elegans, and
C. fasciculatum. Zones 9–11

Chilopsis spp. Desert willow, including *Chilopsis
linearis*. Zones 8–11

Citrus spp. Citrus trees, including orange,
lemon, grapefruit trees. Zones 9–11

Costus spp. Spiral gingers, including
C. pulverulentus and C. speciosus. Zones 9–11

Cuphea spp. Cigar plant or firecracker plant,
including C. ignea and C. micropetala.
Zones 9–11

Delonix regia Flame tree or royal poinciana.
Zones 9–11

Erythrina crista-galli Cockspur coral tree.
Zones 9–11

Erythrina spp. Coral trees, including
E. crista-galli and E. x bidwillii. Zones 8–11

Eucalyptus spp. Eucalyptus or gum tree.
Zones 9–11

Feijoa sellowiana Pineapple guava. Zones 8–11

Fouquieria splendens Ocotillo. Zones 8–11

Fuchsia spp. Fuchsias. Zones 9–11

Hamelia patens Scarlet bush. Zones 9–11

Fledychium spp. Ginger lilies, including
H. aurantiacum and H. coccineum.
Zones 8–11

Heliconia spp. False bird-of-paradise, including *H. brasiliensis*, *H. latispatha*, and *H. schiedeana*. Zones 9–11

Hesperaloe parviflora Red yucca. Zones 6–10

Hibiscus rosa-sinensis Hibiscus. Zones 9–11

Ipomosis aggregata Scarlet gilia. Zones 7–11

Justicia spp. Shrimp plant, Chuparosa, including *J. brandegeana* and *J. californica*. Zones 8–11

Lantana spp. Lantana, shrub verbena, including *L. camara* and *L. montevidensis*. Zones 9–11

Melaleuca spp. Bottlebrushes. Zones 10–11

Nerium oleander Common oleander. Zones 8–11

Nicotiana glauca Tree tobacco. Zones 9–11

Pentas lanceolata Egyptian star cluster. Zones 9–11

Quisqualis indica Rangoon creeper. Zones 9–11

Ruellia graecizans Red ruellia. Zones 9–11

Russelia equisetiformis Fountain bush. Zones 8–11

Sesbaina spp. Scarlet wisteria tree, including *S. grandiflora*, *S. punicea*, and *S. tripetii*. Zones 8–11

Yucca elata Soaptree yucca. Zones 8–11

Zauschneria californica California fuchsia. Zones 8–11

VINES

Antigonon leptopus Coral vine. Zones 8–10

Bignonia capreolata Cross vine or trumpet flower. Zones 6–10

Disticitis buccinatoira Blood-red trumpet vine. Zones 10–11

Pyrostegia venusta Flame vine. Zones 10–11

Tecomaria capensis Cape honeysuckle. Zones 10–11

Tropaeolum speciosum Vermillion nasturtium. Zones 7–9

Lantana (*Lantana camera* 'Lucky Peach').

Scarlet bush (*Hamelia patens*).

Fountain bush (*Russelia equisetiformis*).

Tree tobacco (*Nicotiana glauca*).

Flame vine (*Pyrostegia venusta*).

hummingbird profiles

IN THIS SECTION you'll find profiles for the 15 most commonly encountered hummingbird species found in North America north of the Mexican border. Each profile includes the species name and Latin name, the species' size, measured from bill tip to tail tip, a range map, and a photograph. The text includes sections on the species' description, the important field marks, sounds, behavior, and preferred habitat.

All of these species visit both flowering plants and feeders, but some are more widely distributed and common than others. The range maps give seasonal distribution and range for each species, which can be an important clue to a hummingbird's identification. While hummingbirds can be found far from their expected ranges, especially in fall and winter, such vagrant birds are very rare.

KEY TO RANGE MAPS

SUMMER RANGE

WINTER RANGE

YEAR-ROUND RANGE

– – – APPROXIMATE LIMITS OF SUMMER RANGE

– – – APPROXIMATE LIMITS OF WINTER RANGE

– – – APPROXIMATE LIMITS OF YEAR-ROUND RANGE

LAMPORNIS
CLEMENCIAE
SIZE: 5"

BLUE-THROATED HUMMINGBIRD

description

A large and aggressive hummingbird found in summer in limited parts of southwest Texas, southwest New Mexico, and southeastern Arizona. This large hummingbird appears long-tailed and short-billed.

field marks

The male's bright blue gorget can be hard to see in poor light. Better field marks are this species' large size, white eye stripe, and dark tail with outer feathers broadly tipped in white. The upper back is green, the lower black greenish bronze. The female is identical to the male but with a plain gray throat.

sounds

Highly vocal, making a variety of sounds. Calls include a sharp *seet* note and buzzy trills. Song of male includes a long series of notes on a similar tone given from a perch.

behavior

Highly aggressive and territorial, attacking other hummingbirds, hawks, and owls. Flicks tail while flying or foraging.

habitat

Rarely found outside its preferred habitat of thickly forested mountain streams and moist canyons.

EUGENES
FULGENS

SIZE: 5¼"

RIVOLI'S HUMMINGBIRD

description

The adult male is stunning when seen in direct light. This large hummingbird is not aggressive, despite its size. It is fairly uncommon in the southwestern mountains along the Mexican border.

field marks

The adult male has a purple crown, turquoise gorget, and black chest and belly. A small white spot behind the eye contrasts with the black face. Females are drab by comparison but share the white spot behind the eye, as well as a white eye line. Both sexes are dark green above.

sounds

Calls include harsh *cheep* notes, sometimes in pairs, plus sputters and whistles. Song is a mixture of hisses, sputters, chips, and gurgles.

behavior

Mainly an insect-eater, this magnificent hummingbird is what's known as a "trapline" forager. It moves along a regular route, foraging for insects and some flower nectar, but does not claim and defend a territory based on food sources.

habitat

Found in "sky island" habitat in Arizona, New Mexico, and Texas: mixed pine-oak and riparian forests in mountains above 5,000 feet.

CALOTHORAX
LUCIFER
SIZE: 3½"

LUCIFER HUMMINGBIRD

description

Named not for the devil but for the Greek word for "light-bearer," which refers to its large gorget. The Lucifer is small and slim with a long black decurved bill and a long tail. When perched, it gives a hunched appearance. It is one of the most difficult hummingbird species to see in the U.S.

field marks

Adult males have a large purple-magenta gorget with a ragged lower edge, white breast, and greenish bronze back. Sides show light rufous. Females are greenish above and white below with varying amounts of light rufous on the breast and belly. The tail is long and forked.

sounds

Calls are soft, dry *chip notes*. The male's song is a soft squeak given in territorial disputes. Tail and wing feathers make sounds during dive displays.

behavior

Aggressively territorial. Rarely fans tail, even in flight. Males perform both shuttle and dive displays for females, often at their nest sites.

habitat

Shrubby foothills and canyons, wooded streams, and dry washes of southeastern Arizona, southwestern Texas, and southwestern New Mexico.

ARCHILOCHUS
COLUBRIS
SIZE: 3¾"

RUBY-THROATED HUMMINGBIRD

description

The rubythroat is the only common hummingbird of the East in spring and summer. Most rubythroats leave for the Neotropics in winter, though a few overwinter in the Gulf states. In fall and winter, any hummingbird visiting a feeder should be carefully checked—it may be a vagrant species from the West.

field marks

Adult males have a ruby gorget, which can appear black in bright sunlight, and a black chin strap above the gorget. The chest is pale, the belly greenish, and the crown, back, and tail iridescent green. Females and young birds are green above, white below.

sounds

Calls are high squeaky or sputtering notes. The male's wings hum or whine in display flights.

behavior

May flick its tail occasionally when hovering at flower or feeder. Other food sources include flying insects and sap at sapsucker wells. Bathes in rain, mist from birdbaths, or on water-soaked leaves.

habitat

Usually seen at or near flowering plants, vines, and trees in gardens, woodland edges, and backyards.

ARCHILOCHUS
ALEXANDRI
SIZE: 3¾″

BLACK-CHINNED HUMMINGBIRD

description

This is the most widespread hummingbird in the West. The male's gorget flashes deep purple at the bottom in the right light; in poor light it can appear black.

field marks

Both sexes are bright green on the head, back, and tail. Males show a clean white bib below the dark purple gorget. Females look similar to female ruby-throated hummingbirds.

sounds

The wings of adult males make a dry buzz in flight. Chasing birds give a series of twitters and buzzes. Call is a soft *chew!*

behavior

This species pumps its tail consistently while hovering. Courting males perform both a U-shaped dive display and a back-and-forth shuttle display (a series of short zipping flights back and forth) for perched females. Both displays are accompanied by vocal or wing sounds.

habitat

Common in wooded foothills and canyons and along the Pacific Coast.

ANNA'S HUMMINGBIRD

description

The male Anna's is our only hummingbird with a bright magenta to cherry red crown. This species is common along the Pacific Coast all year long.

field marks

The male's crown and gorget are brilliant ruby in good light but can appear black in poor light. At 4 inches in length, the Anna's is larger than most other widespread western hummingbirds.

sounds

A series of raspy notes and chattery buzzes is what passes for the Anna's song, which the male usually delivers while perched.

behavior

Males can erect gorget and head feathers and move back and forth to flash bright colors at intruders, rivals, and potential mates. While hovering, the Anna's does not pump its tail, unlike many other common hummingbird species.

habitat

Common in brushy habitat in the westernmost states. Any habitat with nectar-producing flowers can host this species.

COSTA'S HUMMINGBIRD

CALYPTE COSTAE
SIZE: 3½"

description

Male Costa's hummingbirds have a striking, deep purple crown and a gorget that extends downward like a mustache. This small hummingbird has a diagnostic call—see below.

field marks

The male's gorget shape and color are unique among our hummingbirds. The female is green above and white below. This species is similar to the black-chinned hummingbird, which is slightly larger. The male black-chinned lacks the extended gorget and purple crown of the male Costa's.

sounds

Call is a high-pitched, tinny *tink-tink-tink-tink*. Male's song and dive display sound is a rising, then falling *ziiiing!*

behavior

Males sing from a prominent perch within their breeding territories and as they perform elaborate looping courtship flights for perched females. These flights may include more than 35 vertical loops above a watching female.

habitat

Desert scrub, chaparral, dry washes with flowering plants, backyards, and gardens.

SELASPHORUS
PLATYCERCUS
SIZE: 4″

BROAD-TAILED HUMMINGBIRD

description

The wings of the adult male produce a loud, whistled trill as he flies. This is the most commonly encountered hummer in the Rocky Mountains.

field marks

Males and females are metallic green above with a white breast and belly. Males have a magenta gorget with no black chin strap. Females have a speckled throat and buffy sides. Both sexes are longer and slimmer than the ruby-throated hummingbird of the East.

sounds

In addition to the wing trill of the male in flight, broad-taileds produce high-pitched chattering calls, usually from a perch. Call is a loud *chit!*

behavior

This relatively unaggressive hummingbird frequently gets dominated by other species at feeders. Returns early to breeding habitat and survives on sap at tree holes and on insects until flower nectar is available. The male performs a bouncing shuttle display in front of the perched female.

habitat

Mountain forests, meadows, and wooded canyons.

SELASPHORUS RUFUS
SIZE: 3¾"

RUFOUS HUMMINGBIRD

description

Rusty, red, and white overall, this is our only North American hummingbird with an all-rufous back. Only males can be separated visually from the very similar Allen's hummingbird. Female rufous and Allen's hummingbirds are indistinguishable.

field marks

The male usually has an entirely rufous back and tail, bright red gorget, and white chest. Some males have extensive green, similar to Allen's hummingbird male.

sounds

Makes a variety of vocal chips and twitters. The male's wings whine in flight, especially during courtship display.

behavior

The rufous hummingbird aggressively defends food sources, even against larger birds. This species is increasingly regular as a fall and winter vagrant to feeders and gardens in the East and Southeast. Males perform an oval-shaped dive display accompanied by loud, descending sputtering calls and snapping sounds from flared feathers.

habitat

Forests, woodland edges, mountain meadows, gardens, backyards, parks.

SELASPHORUS
SASIN
SIZE: 3¾"

ALLEN'S HUMMINGBIRD

description

This rufous, green, and white hummingbird is found along the Pacific Coast. It is very similar to the more widespread rufous hummingbird. Females of the two species are indistinguishable (except to the birds themselves).

field marks

Males have a bright orange gorget, white belly, green crown and back, and rufous tail. (Male rufous hummingbirds have a mostly rufous back and tail.)

sounds

In flight, the male's wings make a loud whine. Call is a loud, piercing *kvikk!* The male often gives it during swooping, pendulum courtship display flights.

behavior

The Allen's is less aggressive than the similar-looking rufous hummingbird but is still territorial around food sources. The male's J-shaped dive display is used both for courtship and in aggressive encounters with rival males. The back-and-forth shuttle display is performed by the male toward the female.

habitat

Woodlands, wooded parks, brushy gardens, backyards.

CALLIOPE HUMMINGBIRD

SELASPHORUS CALLIOPE
SIZE: 3¼"

description

This is the smallest bird in North America north of Mexico. A common visitor to feeders and gardens within its range, the Calliope sometimes holds its tail cocked upward while hovering to feed.

field marks

The male's gorget of magenta feathers may be flared open or held together, forming an inverted V on the throat. The male is green above, white below. The female is green above and white-bellied with buffy flanks. Calliopes look very short-tailed and small compared with other hummingbirds.

sounds

Despite its name, this species is not very vocal. It makes various chips and twitters in flight. The male gives a high-pitched *tsee-see* in courtship flight.

behavior

Often visits flowers very low to the ground. The male performs a U-shaped dive display in courtship, which finishes with a loud *zit-ziing* and a flaring of the brilliant gorget feathers. Shorter shuttle displays may involve both male and female.

habitat

Mountain meadows and open canyons. Often found near water. Present in summer only, though a few winter in the Gulf Coast states.

BROAD-BILLED HUMMINGBIRD

CYNANTHUS
LATIROSTRIS

SIZE: 4"

description

This small and mild-mannered hummer has a very limited range in the South-west. The male is richly colorful with a deep blue gorget and green body and has an orange bill tipped in black. In poor light, however, he may appear all dark.

field marks

The blue and green male has an obvious two-toned bill and a long, notched tail. The female is green above and grayish white below with an obvious white eye stripe that broadens behind the eye. Her bill is mostly dark.

sounds

Vocal sounds include actual singing by males from a prominent perch, described as *jeejeejeejeejee* broken up by scattered chips. Calls are harsh *chit* notes, sometimes given in a series. During the male's pendulum display flights, his wings make a high whine.

behavior

Notably less aggressive than many other species. It twitches its tail while flying or foraging.

habitat

Wooded canyons and shrubby foothills of southeastern Arizona and south-western New Mexico.

AMAZILIA
YUCATANENSIS
SIZE: 4¼"

BUFF-BELLIED HUMMINGBIRD

description

This large hummingbird is well named for its obvious buff belly patch. It is a primarily Neotropical species that is expanding its range northward along the Texas Gulf Coast.

field marks

Iridescent green on the head and throat contrasts with a tan belly and rufous tail and wings. The bill is coral-red tipped in black. Sexes are similar, but the male is slightly more colorful overall.

sounds

A very vocal species. It gives a variety of calls, including harsh *chik* notes and a nasal *mew*. Aggressive calls include a long staticlike rattle. Males sing a complex burbling song, often from cover.

behavior

Males are highly aggressive, especially toward rival males. Flicks tail irregularly in flight. The male's dive display may be accompanied by whirring or whistling wings.

habitat

Coastal scrub and woodlands from the lower Rio Grande Valley northward. Increasingly common at feeding stations in residential areas. Some birds move north and east along the Gulf Coast in winter, reaching as far as Florida.

AMAZILIA
VIOLICEPS
SIZE: 4½"

VIOLET-CROWNED HUMMINGBIRD

description

Bright white below with a dark green-brown back and a bright orange bill, this medium-sized hummingbird is very aggressive at feeders and food plants. It is distributed very locally in southeasternmost Arizona and southwestern New Mexico.

field marks

Sexes look identical. The bright white throat, chest, and belly contrast with the orange bill tipped in black. The crown is dark blue, and upperparts are green fading to brown near the tail.

sounds

Song is more musical than that of other hummingbirds, consisting of four to six *chew* notes descending in pitch. Calls are hard, sputtering *chip* notes, often given in aggressive encounters.

behavior

Aggressively chases other hummingbirds. Males sing from a prominent perch, often early in the day.

habitat

Breeds in streamside woods. Forages in areas with thick vegetation.

WHITE-EARED HUMMINGBIRD

description

A medium-small species irregularly found north of the U.S.-Mexico border in the Southwest.

field marks

The broad white eye stripe that gives the species its name is obvious in all ages and sexes. Males have a black face, short bill with black tip and red base, and a white central patch on the greenish breast. The greenish color of the gorget extends onto the upper sides and flanks.

sounds

Call is a sharp metallic *chink!* Song is a series of call notes with occasional rising trills.

behavior

Aggressive around nectar sources. Both sexes participate in courtship display flights, which involve chases.

habitat

Uncommon in mountains of southeastern Arizona, southwestern New Mexico, and western Texas in pine-oak woodlands between 4,500 and 10,000 feet. Moves to lower elevations in winter.

ATTRACTING BUTTERFLIES

chapter four

Butterflies bring a whole new dimension to a garden. Not only do they add color that flutters and dances over your beds and borders, but watching and learning about them can become a fascinating lifelong hobby. The plants that attract butterflies are easy to incorporate into any garden, because they include so many beloved annuals, perennials, and herbs. Asters, marigolds, sunflowers, and zinnias are just some of the common flowers that butterflies visit.

To plan and plant a butterfly garden, it helps to know a bit about their life cycles. Attracting adult butterflies is the objective of everyone who plants a butterfly garden, but simply dotting a few well-known butterfly flowers around your yard won't necessarily lead to success. You'll have better luck if you take their entire cycle into consideration.

Reproduction is the main goal of all adult butterflies. In fact, some adult butterflies do not feed at all; they simply mate, lay eggs, and die. (You can attract even these species by growing the plants they lay eggs on.) Many, of

Blazing stars or gay-feathers (*Liatris* spp.) are native wildflowers in the daisy family. They attract visitors such as this eastern tiger swallowtail as well as hummingbirds.

Several species of swallowtails lay their eggs on members of the parsley family. This is a black swallowtail caterpillar feeding on dill.

course, visit flowers to sip nectar in the course of finding a mate and laying eggs. Others feed on sap running from tree wounds, rotting fruit, or even scat (animal droppings) and carrion.

Successful butterfly gardens include plants for butterfly larvae, or caterpillars, as well as nectar for adults, and that's where things can get a little complicated. Some species require a specific type of plant for their larvae. Monarch butterflies will lay eggs only on milkweeds (*Asclepias* spp.), for example. Pipevine swallowtails need pipevines, or Dutchman's pipes (*Aristolochia* spp.). Zebra swallowtails lay only on pawpaws (*Asimina* spp.) and related plants. Gulf fritillaries prefer passionflowers (*Passiflora* spp.) Other species are less particular. The American painted lady lays eggs on a wide variety of plants in the aster family, Asteraceae. Viceroys lay on willows, poplars, and a range of fruit trees. Western tiger swallowtails lay on sycamores, willows, poplars, and aspens. The best approach is to include an assortment of plants for larvae; if you have a specific species you would like to attract, plant host plants for that species. Field guides are a good source of information on host plants for each species.

Once the eggs hatch, the larvae, or caterpillars, become world-class eating machines. They consume plant leaves and stems at an enormous rate and grow at amazing speeds. (At this stage, butterfly gardening can seem at odds with the goals of a conventional garden, especially when the caterpillars are chomping on cabbages or parsley.) The caterpillars molt several times as they grow, eventually molting a final time to form a chrysalis. It is during the chrysalis stage that nearly all of the caterpillar's tissues are broken down and transformed. The end result, when the chrysalis opens, is a butterfly. Newly emerged butterflies have fat bodies and wrinkled wings; they have to pump the fluid from their bodies into their wings, causing the wings to expand. Once the wings have dried and stiffened, the new butterfly is ready to fly.

Several generations of butterflies are born each season. At the end of the summer, butterflies have a variety of strategies for overwintering. Some overwinter as eggs and chrysalises—often in leaf litter or attached to host plants. There are also species that roll themselves in leaves and overwinter as caterpillars; others hibernate as adults in buildings and tree hollows. Some simply die off in the North and repopulate their northern ranges from southern populations that gradually move northward during the course of the summer. Monarchs migrate south each fall to overwinter in central Mexico and Southern California. Other species, including painted ladies and buckeyes, also migrate on a limited basis.

Joe-Pye weed (*Eupatorium fistulosum*) attracts an abundance of swallowtails and other butterflies when it flowers in the fall.

TIPS FOR SUCCESS

Leaving a weedy patch or two in your yard can be an ideal strategy for increasing butterfly populations. The larvae of painted ladies feed on burdock (*Arctium lappa*). Several species, including buckeyes and variegated fritillary, visit plantains to lay eggs. Nettles (*Urtica* spp.) host the larvae of Milbert's tortoiseshell, question marks, and red admirals. Common milkweed (*Asclepias syriaca*), thistles (*Cirsium* spp.), dock (*Rumex* spp.), Queen Anne's lace (*Daucus carota*), and beggar ticks (*Bidens* spp.) are other suitable plants for a weedy butterfly nursery.

Many species of skippers are attracted to grasses, including bluegrass, Bermuda grass (*Cynodon dactylon*), panic grass (*Panicum* spp.), and sedges (*Carex* spp.), which can be allowed to grow in a weedy area.

butterfly garden features

START YOUR BUTTERFLY GARDEN IN A SUNNY SPOT that is protected from prevailing winds. A barrier planting of trees and shrubs is ideal; butterflies will appreciate a relatively windless spot where they can fly without being buffeted about. Trellised vines, and even tall annuals or perennials, can also help cut down on wind. In addition to planting butterfly-attracting plants in beds and borders, use them along woodland edges, meadow plantings, and in front of foundation shrubs.

Be sure to include both flowers for nectar and plants for larvae. Try to plant flowers that will bloom in spring, summer, and fall to provide nectar sources all season. Perennials will produce a wide variety of flowers and a progression of blooms. Adding long-blooming annuals will help ensure a steady supply of nectar all summer long.

Here are some other features you can include to make "your" butterflies feel at home.

Single-flowered hollyhocks are attractive to a wide variety of nectar-seeking butterflies.

SUNNING SPOTS

Butterflies will use areas covered with low ground covers, grasses, or clovers to sun themselves. Since they are cold-blooded, sunning helps them regulate their temperatures. Providing a flat rock in a sunny, windless spot along the edge of your butterfly garden is also a good idea.

WATER

There are several ways to provide butterflies with water. A conventional birdbath or other shallow container that is filled with flat stones can provide a safe drinking spot. The stones should emerge from the water, allowing butterflies to alight and drink without getting wet. A low spot that remains moist, or that you keep moist by regular watering, also provides a suitable drinking spot. Butterflies will also visit muddy or sandy spots along streams and pools.

Swallowtail butterflies probe the mud for salt and other nutrients.

VARYING ENVIRONMENTS

The more types of habitats your yard provides, the more species of butterflies you are likely to attract. Boggy areas, shady wooded areas, woodland edges, sunny meadows, and conventional beds and borders will all attract butterflies.

flowers for butterflies

BUTTERFLIES VISIT LITERALLY THOUSANDS OF DIFFERENT PLANTS, both to sip nectar and to lay their eggs. A few plant families are especially important to them, however, either as nectar sources, larval plants, or both. If you include some plants from each of the families described next, you will increase your chances of attracting a variety of butterflies. See "More Flowers for Butterflies" on page 202 for a list of additional butterfly plants that do not belong to the plant families listed next.

Eastern tailed blue
(shown actual size)

Even the common oxeye daisy will provide food for welcome visitors, such as this American lady.

DAISIES

Many kinds of butterflies visit members of the aster family, Asteraceae, looking for nectar. These include sulphurs, question marks, painted ladies, skippers, buckeyes, and fritillaries. Daisies aren't as important as larval plants, but painted ladies, pearl crescents, and blues do use them as food for their larvae. Songbirds also visit the plants for seed in winter, and hummingbirds visit many species for nectar.

The late-summer-to-fall flowers of wild and cultivated asters, including New England aster (*Aster novae-angliae*) and New York aster

Large-flowered tickseed (*Coreopsis grandiflora*) produces a bounty of butterfly-attracting flowers from late spring through summer.

(*A. novae-beglii*), feature characteristic daisy flowers with yellow centers and purple, white, or pink ray florets. They provide an important nectar source for adults, along with other late-blooming aster-family members, including sneezeweed (*Helenium autumnale*), annual and perennial sunflowers (*Helianthus* spp.), and goldenrods (*Solidago* spp.).

Summer-blooming daisies for a butterfly garden include coreopsis or tickseed (*Coreopsis* spp.), annual and perennial cornflowers (*Centaurea* spp.), oxeye daisies (*Chrysanthemum leucanthemum*), Shasta daisy (*C. maximum*), oxeye (*Heliopsis helianthoides*), fleabanes (*Erigeron* spp.), blanket flowers (*Gaillardia* spp.), senecios or groundsels (*Senecio* spp.), black-eyed Susans (*Rudbeckia* spp.), and purple coneflowers (*Echinacea* spp.).

Yarrow (*Achillea* spp.), Joe-Pye weed (*Eupatorium* spp.), hardy ageratum (*Ageratum houstonianum*), and ironweed (*Vernonia* spp.) also are members of this large family, although their clusters of tiny blooms

Purple coneflower (*Echinacea purpurea*) is a tough, easy-to-grow wildflower that thrives in sun and blooms all summer.

don't look particularly asterlike. Gayfeathers (*Liatris* spp.) bear tall stalks of flowers covered with woolly-looking flowers.

In addition to annual sunflowers, several other popular annuals belong to this group and make great additions to a butterfly garden. The following plants are ideal for providing a summer-long supply of flowers: cornflowers or bachelor's button (*Centaurea cyanus*), cosmos (*Cosmos* spp.), Mexican hat (*Ratibida columnifera*), Mexican sunflowers (*Tithonia rotundifolia*), marigolds (*Tagetes* spp.), and zinnias (*Zinnia* spp.).

Several aster family members that are considered weeds also attract butterflies. Consider growing them in meadows, along fencerows, or in other appropriate areas. These include beggar ticks (*Bidens* spp.), hawkweeds (*Hieracium* spp.), dandelions (*Taraxacum officinale*), and thistles (*Cirsium* spp.).

It would be difficult indeed to plan a flower garden—much less a butterfly garden—without including some members of this large tribe. They're beloved additions to beds, borders, and meadows everywhere. Most species thrive in full sun with average to rich soil that is well drained.

PEAS, CLOVERS, AND OTHER LEGUMES

Members of the pea family, Fabaceae, are good nectar sources for many butterflies, but should also be included in every butterfly garden because they are important plants for butterfly larvae. Sulphurs, blues, and skippers are among the butterflies that use them as food for their larvae. Conventional garden plants that fall into this family include sweet peas

(*Lathyrus* spp., including perennial pea, *L. latifolius*) and lupines (*Lupinus* spp.).

Alfalfa (*Medicago sativa*) and clovers (sweet clovers, *Melilotus* spp., and *Trifolium* spp.) are both good nectar plants.

Several leguminous trees, shrubs, and vines host butterfly larvae and adults, including false indigo (*Amorpha* spp.), senna or shower tree (*Cassia* spp.), locusts (*Robinia* spp.), indigo-bushes (*Dalea* spp.), indigos (*Indigofera* spp.), mesquite (*Prosopis* spp.), redbuds (*Cercis* spp.), and wisterias (*Wisteria* spp.). Beans, including scarlet runner beans (*Phaseolus coccineus*), which also attract hummingbirds, and broad beans (*Vicia faba*) and other vetches, including *Vicia* spp., crown vetch (*Coronilla varia*), and milk vetch (*Astragalus* spp.), are also in this family.

Most legumes thrive in full sun with average to poor soil. All have the ability to fix atmospheric nitrogen, so they will grow well even in soil that is not very fertile.

Red clover (*Trifolium pratense*) is a common meadow inhabitant that attracts swallowtails and a variety of other butterflies.

Lavender (*Lavandula angustifolia*)

MINTS

Members of the mint family, Lamiaceae, feature square stems and spikes of small, two-lipped flowers that attract both butterflies and beneficial insects. The pungent leaves of many mints make them beloved herb garden plants. These include true mints (*Mentha* spp.), hyssops (*Agastache* spp.), lavenders (*Lavandula* spp.), catnip and catmints (*Nepeta* spp.), rosemary (*Rosmarinus officinalis*), and thymes (*Thymus* spp.). Prunella (*Prunella vulgaris*) is a mint family ground cover. Two mints are also essential hummingbird garden plants: bee balm (*Monarda* spp.) and sages and salvias (*Salvia* spp.). Both are as at home in the herb garden as they are in the flower garden.

Mints thrive in full sun. Most prefer rich, moist, well-drained soil. Many mints are vigorous plants that can quickly overtake a garden. Grow true mints, hyssops, and bee balms in a spot where their spreading won't pose problems. Or, to control their wandering roots, plant them in bottomless buckets or tubs sunk in the soil.

MILKWEEDS

Monarch butterflies are perhaps the best-known visitors to members of the milkweed family, Asclepiadaceae, but many other species dine on their nectar as well, including swallowtails, sulphurs, fritillaries, painted ladies, viceroys, skippers, and question marks. Queens also lay eggs on milkweeds. Perhaps the best-known garden flower in the milkweed family is butterfly weed, *Asclepias tuberosa*, which fits as nicely in meadows and wild gardens as it does in borders. Other cultivated milkweeds include bloodflower (*A. curassavica*), an annual, as well as swamp milkweed (*A. incarnata*) and showy milkweed, both perennials.

Most milkweeds require full sun with average loamy or sandy soil that is well drained. Swamp milkweed will survive in dry soil, but prefers evenly moist conditions.

Butterfly weed
(*Asclepias tuberosa*)

Bloodflower (*Asclepias curassavica*) is a tender perennial milkweed that can be grown as an annual. Monarchs lay their eggs on its leaves.

Painted lady (shown actual size)

Black swallowtail
(shown actual size)

PARSLEYS

Plants in the parsley or carrot family, Apiaceae, are especially attractive to swallowtails. Eastern black swallowtails and anise swallowtails, as well as several other species, lay their eggs on parsley (*Petroselinum crispum*), dill (*Anethum graveolens*), and Queen Anne's lace (*Daucus carota*). Both Eastern black swallowtails and gray hairstreaks visit the flowers of Queen Anne's lace for nectar. Fennel (*Foeniculum vulgare*) and wild parsnip (*Pastinaca sativa*) are two other members of this family.

Grow parsley family members in full sun in average to rich, well-drained soil. Be sure to plant enough for both you and the butterflies to enjoy. Protect dill and parsley plants you want to keep for

Dill is one member of the parsley family that swallowtail larvae feed on. Others are parsley, Queen Anne's lace, and fennel.

your own harvest with floating row covers or netting to keep adults from laying eggs on them. Or gently move larvae you spot on your own plants to butterfly plantings of the same species or to Queen Anne's lace or wild parsnip plants growing nearby.

VIOLETS AND PANSIES

Violets and pansies make charming additions to any garden and are especially useful in a garden designed to attract butterflies. Several species of fritillaries lay eggs on these diminutive plants, and spring azures visit the flowers for nectar. Canada violet *(Viola canadensis)*, sweet violet *(V. odorata)*, and horned violet *(V. cornuta)* are all popular garden perennials.

Violets will grow in sun or shade and prefer a spot with moist soil that is rich in humus. They can become invasive because they self-sow with abandon.

Gulf fritillary (shown actual size)

MORE FLOWERS FOR BUTTERFLIES

Butterflies visit a wide range of flowers for nectar. Here are some more flowers to consider for your butterfly garden. A bird symbol indicates that hummingbirds will also visit the flowers.

ANNUALS

Antirrhinum spp. Snapdragons

Cleome hasslerana Spider flower

Dianthus barbatus Sweet William

Miriabilis jalapa Four-o'clocks, marvel of Peru

Nicotiana alata Flowering tobacco

Petunia spp. Petunias

PERENNIALS

Alcea a rosea Hollyhocks

Allium spp. Onions, garlic

Astilbe spp. Astilbe

Camassia spp. Camassia

Campanula spp. Bellflowers

Centranthus ruber Jupiter's beard, red valerian

Dianthus spp. Pinks

Eriogonum spp. Buckwheats

Filipendula spp. Queen of the prairie

Geranium spp. Hardy geraniums

Heliotropium arborescens Heliotrope, cherry pie

Hemerocallis spp. Daylilies

Hibiscus spp. Hibiscus

Lantana spp. Lantanas

Limonium spp. Sea lavenders

Lobelia spp. Cardinal flower, lobelia

Penstemon spp. Penstemons

Phlox spp. Phlox

Scabiosa spp. Sweet scabious

Sedum spp. Sedum, especially *S. spectabile*

Thalictrum spp. Thalictrum, meadow rue

Yucca spp. Yucca, Adam's needle

A monarch on showy sedum (*Sedum spectabile*).

Dame's rocket (*Hesperis matronalis*)

Butterflies visit the flowers of several species of buckeyes. This is bottlebrush buckeye (*Aesculus parviflora*), a spreading shrub that reaches about 10 feet in height.

Queen (shown actual size)

MUSTARDS AND OTHER CRUCIFERS

The mustard family, Brassicaceae, presents something of a battleground between the goals of conventional gardening and butterfly gardening. As its name suggests, the cabbage white butterfly feeds on cabbages and many other members of the mustard family, including broccoli, cauliflower, and kale. Other species of whites and long-tailed skippers visit other mustard family members, including basket-of-gold (*Aurinia saxatilis*), sea kale (*Crambe maritima*), wallflowers (*Cherianthus* spp.), dame's rocket (*Hesperis matronalis*), and sweet alyssum (*Lobularia maritima*).

Use floating row covers to keep adult butterflies from laying eggs on cabbages and other crops. Simply spread the row covers loosely over the plants at planting time. "Tuck in" the edges all around with soil to prevent pests from getting access to the plants.

trees, shrubs, and vines for butterflies

BUTTERFLIES VISIT MANY DIFFERENT TREES, SHRUBS, AND VINES, both for nectar and to lay eggs. In fact, some of the most important plants for butterfly larvae are trees. Willows (*Salix* spp.) and aspens and poplars (*Populus* spp.) host the larvae of western tiger swallowtails, mourning cloaks, white admirals, red-spotted purples, and viceroys. Hackberries (*Celtis* spp.) host hackberry butterflies, as well as question marks and mourning cloaks. Honeysuckles (*Lonicera* spp.), sweet pepperbush (*Clethra alnifolia*), mock oranges (*Philadelphus* spp.), pink azalea (*Rhododendron periclymenoides*), and elderberries (*Sambucus* spp.) are especially good sources of nectar.

You may already be growing some of the species listed below; many are also important to songbirds and hummingbirds. A flower symbol ✿ indicates a species that is used both for nectar and as food for larvae.

Aesculus spp. Buckeyes

Alnus spp. Alders

Amelanchier spp. Serviceberries

Aristolochia spp. Pipevines, including *A. durior* (Dutchman's pipe) and *A. serpentaria* (Virginia snakeroot)

Asimina spp. Pawpaws

Betula spp. Birches

Buddleia spp. Butterfly bush

Carpinus caroliniana American hornbeam

Caryopteris spp. Bluebeard

Ceanothus spp. Wild lilacs, including New Jersey tea (*C. americanus*), Rocky Mountain wild lilac (*C. fendleri*), blueblossom (*C. thyrsiflorus*), snowbush (*C. cordulatus*), and deerbush (*C. integerrimus*) ✿

Celtis spp. Hackberries ✿

Citrus spp. Citrus

Cornus spp. Dogwoods ✿

Crataegus spp. Hawthorns

Fraxinus spp. Ashes

Hibiscus syriacus Rose of Sharon

Holodiscus spp. Rock spiraea

Humulus lupulus Hops

Ligustrum spp. Privets

Lindera benzoin Spicebush

Liriodendron tulipifera Tulip tree

Magnolia virginiana Sweet bay

Malus spp. Apples and crab apples

Passiflora spp. Passionflowers

Plantago spp. Plantains

Platanus Sycamores

Populus Aspens

Potentilla Cinquefoils, potentillas ✿

Prunus spp. Cherries and plums, including
P. serotina* and *P. virginiana*
Ptelea trifoliata Hop tree
Quercus spp. Oaks
Rhamnus spp. Buckthorns
Rhus spp. Sumacs
Ribes spp. Gooseberries
Robinia spp. Locust trees
Rubus spp. Blackberries and raspberries

Salix spp. Willows
Sassafras albidum Sassafras
Spiraea spp. Spiraea or bridal wreath
Syringa spp. Lilacs
Vaccinium spp. Blueberries
Viburnum spp. Viburnums
Vitex agnus-castus Chaste tree
Zanthoxylum americanum Prickly ash,
also *Z. clava-herculis*, Hercules' club

Buckeye (shown actual size)

Clouded sulphur (shown actual size)

Monarch (shown actual size)

butterfly profiles

ON THE FOLLOWING PAGES you will find brief profiles for 40 common North American butterflies. Each profile provides primary host plants for caterpillars and popular sources of nectar for adults. Life-cycle entries describe what to look for as eggs and caterpillars develop on host plants in your garden. Caterpillars are sometimes difficult to identify, so supplemental pictorial guides may help resolve questions about them. The habitat category lists ecological settings where each species is typically found. The backyard section adds tidbits of useful knowledge for butterfly gardeners. Range maps show areas where each species resides in red and areas occupied seasonally in blue. Yellow dots document sightings outside the normal range. Size gives the typical wingspan, measured from outer wingtip to outer wingtip.

KEY TO RANGE MAPS

RESIDENT

TEMPORARY RESIDENT (OR EXPANDING LOCATION)

EXTRA LIMITAL APPEARANCE OF STRAYS

BATTUS
PHILENOR

SIZE: 2¾–3½″

PIPEVINE SWALLOWTAIL

host plant
Dutchman's pipe, Virginia snakeroot.

nectar plant
Swamp milkweed, phlox, thistle, honeysuckle, azalea, butterfly bush.

life cycle
Eggs are tan, in clusters. Caterpillar is black with black (or red) spines and red warts.

habitat
Meadows, fields, canyons, forest edges, pine woods.

backyard
Range is expanding. Frequently seen in gardens, orchards, and near water.

PAPILIO
POLYXENES
SIZE: 2¾–3½"

BLACK SWALLOWTAIL

host plant
Parsley, dill, fennel, carrot, Queen Anne's lace.

nectar plant
Ironweed, milkweed, mistflower, phlox, thistle, butterfly bush.

life cycle
Eggs are yellow. Young caterpillar mimics bird dropping. Mature caterpillar is green or white with yellow spots on black bands.

habitat
Old-fields, meadows, farmland, near water.

backyard
Caterpillars frequently dine on parsley or carrot in vegetable and herb gardens.

PAPILIO ZELICAON

SIZE: 2½–3″

ANISE SWALLOWTAIL

host plant
Carrot, cow parsnip, fennel, parsley, citrus.

nectar plant
Mint, penstemon, zinnia, butterfly bush.

life cycle
Eggs are yellow. Caterpillar is green with orange spots in black bands.

habitat
From sea level to mountaintops, sagebrush, canyons, but not in dense woods.

backyard
The most common swallowtail west of the Rocky Mountains; frequents gardens and parks.

PAPILIO
CRESPHONTES
SIZE: 3½–5½″

GIANT SWALLOWTAIL

host plant
Rue, citrus, Hercules' club, hoptree, pricklyash.

nectar plant
Goldenrod, milkweed, lantana, honeysuckle, azalea, citrus.

life cycle
Eggs are dull brown. Caterpillar is splotched brown and buff and resembles bird dropping.

habitat
Fields, forest edges, glades, hammocks, river corridors, citrus groves.

backyard
Most common in South, but can fly long distances and strays widely.

PAPILIO GLAUCUS

SIZE: 3–5½″

EASTERN TIGER SWALLOWTAIL

host plant
Tuliptree, ash, cherry, sweet bay.

nectar plant
Bee balm, red clover, ironweed, milkweed, phlox, thistle, butterfly bush.

life cycle
Eggs are yellow-green. Young caterpillar resembles bird dropping. Mature caterpillar is green-brown with crosswise yellow band, large eyespots. Adult males and some females are yellow with black tiger stripes. Dark-phase females are blue-black with only traces of stripes.

habitat
Woods, shrubby fields, orchards, roadsides, watercourses.

backyard
Widest ranging of the swallowtails; easily seen in gardens and parks.

PAPILIO
TROLIUS
SIZE: 3½–4½"

SPICEBUSH
SWALLOWTAIL

host plant

Spicebush, sassafras.

nectar plant

Cardinal flower, clover, dogbane, ironweed, jewelweed, Joe-Pye weed, milkweed, phlox, thistle, honeysuckle.

life cycle

Green eggs. Tiny caterpillar mimics bird dropping. Humped green adult has large black and yellow eyespots that mimic a snake's head.

habitat

Forest edges, pine barrens, meadows, swamps, watercourses, woodlands.

backyard

Visits gardens, especially those rich in native flowers and shrubs.

ZEBRA SWALLOWTAIL

EURYTIDES MARCELLUS
SIZE: 2¼–3½"

host plant
Pawpaw.

nectar plant
Pickerelweed, milkweed, hardy ageratum, Joe-Pye weed, butterfly bush.

life cycle
Eggs are pale green. Caterpillar is usually green with tiny black dots, one bold black band, and many yellow and white bands. Less common dark form is mostly black.

habitat
Lakeshores, marshes, swamps, watercourses, wooded areas near water.

backyard
Visits gardens that contain, or are located near, pawpaw host plants.

PONTIA
PROTODICE
SIZE: 1¼–2″

CHECKERED WHITE

host plant
Shepherd's purse, winter cress, wild peppergrass, cleome, cabbage.

nectar plant
Aster, dogbane, heliotrope, milkweed, winter cress.

life cycle
Eggs are yellow. Caterpillar is downy bluish green with four lengthwise yellow stripes and numerous black spots with tiny hairs.

habitat
Weedy fields, vacant lots, disturbed areas, sandy places, primarily in low elevations.

backyard
Most common in southern and western U.S. Frequents roadsides, fields, and urban habitats; huge numbers in some years.

SARA ORANGETIP

ANTHOCHARIS SARA

SIZE: 1¼–1¾″

host plant
Rock cress, winter cress, hedge mustard, other mustards (eats flowers, seed pods).

nectar plant
Dandelion, monkeyflower, strawberry, bitter cherry.

life cycle
Egg are yellow to orange. Caterpillar is moss green, stippled with white and dark green.

habitat
From seaside to mountains and deserts; canyons, open areas, ridgetops.

backyard
Attracted to sunny habitats, high or open places. Seen in spring to early summer.

COLIAS
PHILODICE
SIZE: 1½–2"

CLOUDED SULPHUR

host plant
Alfalfa, trefoil, vetch, white clover, white sweetclover.

nectar plant
Aster, clover, dandelion, dogbane, goldenrod, milkweed, phlox, sedum.

life cycle
Eggs are bright green. Green caterpillar has prominent side stripes of white over dark.

habitat
Most open areas except deserts. Abundant in clover and alfalfa fields.

backyard
Originally in eastern North America; has spread widely. Interbreeds with orange sulphur.

**COLIAS
EURYTHEME**

SIZE: 1½–2½″

ORANGE SULPHUR

host plant

Alfalfa, vetch, white clover, white sweetclover, wild indigo.

nectar plant

Alfalfa, aster, clover, coreopsis, heliotrope, thistle, rabbitbrush, redosier dogwood.

life cycle

Eggs are white. Caterpillar is green with adjoining white, pink, and dark side stripes and fine hairs.

habitat

Open areas, especially agricultural fields with alfalfa or clover.

backyard

Abundant and easy to attract to a wide range of host and nectar plants.

PINK-EDGED SULPHUR

COLIAS INTERIOR
SIZE: 1¼–1¾"

host plant
Blueberry.

nectar plant
Aster, bristly sarsaparilla.

life cycle
Pale yellow egg. Caterpillar is bright yellow-green; has light stripes on back and bluish side stripes edged in red.

habitat
Northern bogs, marshes, meadows, clearings, burned areas.

backyard
Males often congregate at moist soil and puddles.

SOUTHERN DOGFACE

COLIAS CESONIA
SIZE: 1¾–2½"

host plant

Clover, false indigo, indigobush, leadplant, prairie clover, soybean.

nectar plant

Alfalfa, aster, butterfly milkweed, coreopsis, thistle, verbena.

life cycle

Egg is white and shaped like a tiny football. Caterpillar is green with a variable light lateral stripe. Mature caterpillars have yellow and black bands and black dots.

habitat

Diverse; uses open woodlands, scrublands, prairies, deserts.

backyard

With wings closed, resembles other sulphurs. Has a bold black-orange design when wings are open.

PHOEBIS
SENNAE
SIZE: 2–2¾"

CLOUDLESS SULPHUR

host plant
Clover, partridge pea, senna.

nectar plant
Cardinal flower, hibiscus, lantana, milkweed, morning glory, thistle, firebush.

life cycle
Eggs are white, turning orange. Caterpillar is green with a yellow side stripe and black dots.

habitat
Forest edges, glades, pinelands, roadsides, swamps, thickets, watercourses.

backyard
Some years see huge late-summer and autumn emigrations into North and West.

EUREMA NICIPPE
SIZE: 1¼–2"

SLEEPY ORANGE

host plant
Clover, senna, other legumes.

nectar plant
Beggar ticks, blue porterweed, sweet alyssum, tickseed sunflower.

life cycle
Eggs are yellow. Caterpillar is downy blue-green; darker below with a light side stripe.

habitat
Old-fields, wet meadows, woodland edges, open pine forests, scrub.

backyard
Visits herb gardens to nectar on chives, lavender, mint, marigold, and oregano.

LYCAENA
PHLAEAS
SIZE: ¾–1¼"

AMERICAN COPPER

host plant
Sheep sorrel, mountain sorrel, curly dock.

nectar plant
Daisy, goldenrod, hardy ageratum, yarrow.

life cycle
Eggs are pale green. Caterpillar is downy, sluglike, and green (or yellow-green or reddish).

habitat
East: Pastures, old-fields, disturbed land. West: mountain slopes, rock-strewn Arctic areas.

backyard
Sheep sorrel and curly dock are considered weeds but will bring caterpillars to your garden, especially in Northeast. Adult butterflies stay low to the ground.

BROWN ELFIN

CALLOPHRYS AUGUSTINUS
SIZE: ¾–1¼″

host plant
Blueberry, bearberry, huckleberry, Labrador tea, leatherleaf, madrone, salal.

nectar plant
Buckwheat, winter cress, heath, bitterbrush, blueberry, wild plum, willow.

life cycle
Eggs are greenish. Caterpillar is bright green, with red and yellow bands when mature.

habitat
Pine barrens, bogs, forest edges, open woodlands, stream banks.

backyard
Widespread in spring; easy to lure with host plants. Also visits moist ground.

GRAY HAIRSTREAK

STRYMON MELINUS
SIZE: 1–1¼″

host plant
Corn, cotton, hops, various legumes, mints, strawberry, oak.

nectar plant
Boneset, butterfly milkweed, goldenrod, mint, sedum, yarrow, verbena, wild lilac.

life cycle
Eggs are pale green. Caterpillar is slug-shaped; often green (pink, red, or brown) with a slightly darker stripe on back and many short hairs on each segment.

habitat
Open spaces, vacant lots, old-fields, roadsides, coastal areas, forest openings.

backyard
Very adaptable and widespread; visits many domestic crop plants and herbs.

EASTERN TAILED-BLUE

EVERES
COMYNTAS
SIZE: ¾–1¼"

host plant
Beans, clovers, lespedeza, lupine, tick trefoil, vetch, wild pea.

nectar plant
Lavender, legumes, mints, oregano, yarrow.

life cycle
Eggs are green. Caterpillar is tiny with downy hairs. Variable green (pink, rose, purple, or yellow-brown) with a darker stripe on back and lower side.

habitat
Open and disturbed areas, such as roadsides, rights of way, old-fields.

backyard
Flies low to the ground. Attracted to weedy patches with wild clover.

SPRING AZURE

host plant
Black snakeroot, meadowsweet, blueberry, wild lilac, viburnum, flowering dogwood.

nectar plant
Coltsfoot, dandelion, forget-me-not, rock cress, violet.

life cycle
Eggs are green. Caterpillar is flattened and wrinkled. Variable green (pink, cream, or brown) with tiny white hairs.

habitat
From shorelines to mountaintops; clearings, brush, open woodlands, glades.

backyard
Visits herb gardens for nectar. Males cluster around damp soil and dung piles.

MORMON METALMARK

APODEMIA
MORMO
SIZE: ¾–1¼"

host plant
Buckwheat.

nectar plant
Desert marigold, groundsel, mustards, rock cress, rabbitbrush.

life cycle
Eggs are pale pink. Tufted caterpillar is gray-purple, darker on back, lighter below.

habitat
From sea level to mountains, usually on open dry areas or rocky slopes.

backyard
Flies low to the ground. Attracted to yellow nectar flowers.

LIBYTHEANA
CARINENTA
SIZE: 1½–2"

AMERICAN SNOUT

host plant
Hackberry, sugarberry.

nectar plant
Mountainmint, verbena, zinnia, butterfly bush, rabbitbrush, dogwood.

life cycle
Eggs are pale green, laid in clusters. Caterpillar is humped, variably colored, with two black tubercles behind head. Most are green with tiny pale spots and a pale side stripe; there is also a dark-phase caterpillar.

habitat
Watercourses, forest edges, thickets, hardwood forests with hackberry trees.

backyard
Can be lured to yards with patches of damp soil. Adults resemble dead leaves when perched.

GULF FRITILLARY

AGRAULIS
VANILLAE
SIZE: 2½–3″

host plant
Passionflower.

nectar plant
Beggar ticks, lantana, passionflower, thistle, Mexican sunflower.

life cycle
Eggs are yellow. Caterpillar is marked with black (or purple) and bright red-orange lengthwise stripes. Body is shiny, with many sharp black spines.

habitat
Old-fields, pastures, thickets, hammocks, forest edges.

backyard
Fairly easy to lure to sunny gardens with passionflower.

GREAT SPANGLED FRITILLARY

host plant
Violet. Caterpillars feed at night.

nectar plant
Black-eyed Susan, milkweed, purple coneflower, thistle, verbena.

life cycle
Eggs are pale brown. Caterpillar is dark; has black branching spines with orange bases. Head is orange and black.

habitat
Meadows, pastures, open woodlands, clearings near conifer forests.

backyard
Tiny caterpillars overwinter near violets. Shelter them with leaf litter.

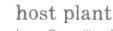

PEARL CRESCENT

PHYCIODES
THAROS
SIZE: 1–1½″

host plant

Aster. Caterpillars feed in small groups.

nectar plant

Aster, beggar ticks, daisy, fleabane, goldenrod, purple coneflower, thistle.

life cycle

Eggs are yellow, in clusters. Caterpillar is dark brown with light speckles; light lines on sides; branched spines emerge from bulbous brown warts. Head is shiny black with white marks.

habitat

Open areas, old-fields, roadsides, damp meadows, stream banks.

backyard

Widespread; easy to lure with asters. Males puddle at moist areas and defend perches.

POLYGONIA INTERROGATIONIS

SIZE: 2¼–2¾"

QUESTION MARK

host plant
Nettle, hops, elm, hackberry.

nectar plant
Carrion, dung, rotting fruit, tree sap.

life cycle
Eggs are green, laid in rows or stacks; may be near, rather than on, host. Caterpillar is black with tiny white speckles; has black spines on head, orange spines and lines on back.

habitat
Open woods, glades, roadsides, stream banks.

backyard
Common near orchards and in suburbs where rotting fruits are available. Especially drawn to rotting crab apples. May become drunk after eating fermented fruit juices.

NYMPHALIS ANTIOPA

SIZE: 2¾–3½"

MOURNING CLOAK

host plant
Birch, cottonwood, elm, hackberry, poplar, willow.

nectar plant
Aphid honeydew, carrion, dung, rotting fruit, tree sap.

life cycle
Eggs are in clusters; olive when laid, turning black. Caterpillar is shiny black with tiny white speckles, red markings in center of back, red legs, and black spines.

habitat
Forest edges, glades, woodland clearings, watercourses.

backyard
Caterpillars feed within a web when small; remain in a group until nearly mature. If frightened, they thrash back and forth in unison. Adults overwinter and are often the first spring butterfly in a garden.

NYMPHALIS
MILBERTI

SIZE: 1¾–2"

MILBERT'S TORTOISESHELL

host plant

Nettle.

nectar plant

Tree sap, wide variety of wildflowers.

life cycle

Eggs are pale green, in clusters. Caterpillar is black with light speckles; has yellow-green markings on back and sides, black branched spines, and stiff white hairs.

habitat

Widely varied, from beaches to mountain slopes and rocky alpine areas; meadows, roadsides, watercourses, weedy places.

backyard

Tiny caterpillars gather in silken webs; groups defoliate host plants. Older caterpillars are solitary and rest in folded leaves. They are well adapted to cold climates; overwintering adults may bask on warm winter days.

PAINTED LADY

VANESSA CARDUI

SIZE: 2–2¼"

host plant

Thistle. Also borage, burdock, groundsel, hollyhock, knapweed, mallow, pearly everlasting, wormwood.

nectar plant

Aster, blazing star, Joe-Pye weed, ironweed, tickseed sunflower, verbena, zinnia, rabbitbrush, chaste tree.

life cycle

Eggs are pale green. Caterpillar is variable (black, green, yellow, pink, or gray-brown) but always has a black head, fine white hairs, and short branched spines (black, yellow, orange, or buff) with black tips on back. Usually has a dark line flanked by pale stripes on the back and pale side stripes.

habitat

Visits most sunny habitats from deserts and meadows to mountains and suburbs.

backyard

Known as the thistle butterfly because of its favorite host. Similar-looking and closely related West Coast lady is common in West, and American lady is common in East.

VANESSA ATALANTA

SIZE: 1¾–2¼″

RED ADMIRAL

host plant

Stinging nettle, false nettle, wood nettle, hops.

nectar plant

Rotting fruit, tree sap. Aster, beggar ticks, blazing star, goldenrod, milkweed, red clover, thistle, butterfly bush.

life cycle

Eggs are green. Caterpillar is variable, usually black (white or yellow-green) with white flecks. Pale splotches or a pale line on lower side, stiff pale spines on the back; head is black.

habitat

Meadows, fields, forest edges, glades, roadsides, swamps, watercourses, barnyards.

backyard

Caterpillars make shelters at leaf tips or by folding a leaf over themselves. Adults allow close approach; they commonly land on humans.

JUNONIA COENIA
SIZE: 2–2½"

COMMON BUCKEYE

host plant

Plantain, gerardia, Mexican petunia, monkeyflower, snapdragon, toadflax, vervain.

nectar plant

Aster, boneset, dogbane, goldenrod, ironweed, milkweed, mistflower, peppermint, sedum, wild buckwheat.

life cycle

Eggs are dark green. Caterpillar is dark with a pale back stripe and white or orange side markings. Blue-black spines on back; side spines have warty orange bases. Head and prolegs are orange.

habitat

Fields, marshes, meadows, shorelines, swamps, roadsides.

backyard

Caterpillars consume lawn weed plantain. Adults often bask on warm bare ground.

LIMENITIS ARTHEMIS

LIMENITIS ARTHEMIS
ASTYANAX

LIMENITIS ARTHEMIS
ARTHEMIS

SIZE: 3–3½"

RED-SPOTTED ADMIRAL
RED-SPOTTED PURPLE AND WHITE ADMIRAL

Until recently, these were considered separate species. They are now regarded as one species, but are usually described by their distinctive characteristics.

host plant

Apple, aspen, black cherry, hornbeam, and oak for red-spotted purple. Birch, hawthorn, poplar, and willow for white admiral.

nectar plant

Aphid honeydew, carrion, dung, rotting fruit, tree sap, spiraea, viburnum.

life cycle

Eggs are green. Humped caterpillar resembles bird droppings. Brown with creamy saddle marking and a side stripe; has a pair of branched horns behind head.

habitat

Forest edges, meadows, open deciduous woods, shorelines, and watercourses for red-spotted purple. Boreal and mixed hardwood forests and scrubby mountain slopes for white admiral.

backyard

Adult red-spotted purples (southern form) and white admirals (northern form) are distinct color races of the same species. Their caterpillars look alike.

LIMENITIS
ARCHIPPUS
SIZE: 2½–3″

VICEROY

host plant

Apple, aspen, cherry, plum, poplar, willow.

nectar plant

Aphid honeydew, carrion, dung, rotting fruit, aster, beggar ticks, Joe-Pye weed, ironweed, milkweed, thistle, butterfly bush.

life cycle

Eggs are greenish. Caterpillar mimics bird droppings. Brown with creamy saddle marking and side stripe; humped, with a pair of branched horns behind head, spines on back and side of head.

habitat

Marshes, meadows, moist open areas, watercourses.

backyard

Caterpillars hibernate in shredded leaves attached to small branches of host plant. In southern and western areas where monarchs are scarce, viceroys mimic queens.

LIMENITIS
LORQUINI
SIZE: 2¼–3"

LORQUIN'S ADMIRAL

host plant
Aspen, chokecherry, cottonwood, willow.

nectar plant
Bird droppings, dung, fernbush, yerba santa, California buckeye.

life cycle
Eggs are pale green. Tiny caterpillar is dark with a white saddle. Mature caterpillar is mottled olive and brown-buff, with a light side stripe and saddle, and bristly horns. It overwinters in a rolled leaf.

habitat
Widespread from lowlands to mountains. Forest edges, watercourses, damp places.

backyard
Pugnacious; will "attack" passing dragonflies, butterflies, birds, and mammals.

COMMON WOOD-NYMPH

CERCYONIS PEGALA

SIZE: 2–3″

host plant

Beardgrass, bluegrass, bluestem grasses, oatgrass, purpletop grass, redtop grass.

nectar plant

Rotting fruit, tree sap, alfalfa, spiraea.

life cycle

Eggs are yellow. Caterpillar is green or yellow-green with short fuzzy hairs, a darker green stripe on back, and yellow-green side stripes. Tail end has two reddish pink tips.

habitat

Fields, grasslands, meadows, open oak and pine woods, utility rights of way.

backyard

Adult appearance varies regionally, but all are beautifully camouflaged. Look for them sitting quietly on tree bark or branches, where they drink sap.

DANAUS PLEXIPPUS

SIZE: 3½–4"

MONARCH

host plant
Milkweed.

nectar plant
Milkweed, beggar ticks, blazing star, blue mistflower, goldenrod, ironweed, lantana, Mexican sunflower, zinnia, butterfly bush.

life cycle
Eggs are pale yellow. Caterpillar is boldly marked with alternating black, white, and yellow bands; it has a pair of black filaments at each end.

habitat
Weedy fields, meadows, marshes, roadsides, watercourses.

backyard
The most recognizable butterfly in North America. During migration, may be seen from seashores to mountains, in rural areas and suburbs.

DANAUS
GILIPPUS
SIZE: 3–3¼"

QUEEN

host plant
Milkweed, white vine.

nectar plant
Aster, beggar ticks, blue mistflower, butterfly milkweed, fogfruit, heliotrope, ironweed, Mexican sunflower, verbena, zinnia.

life cycle
Eggs are pale. Caterpillar resembles a monarch but with wider black or reddish brown bands. It has paired long black filaments behind head; shorter pairs on back and at rear.

habitat
Coastal areas, fields, glades, hammocks, pine woods, thickets, salt marshes, roadsides in the Southeast; open areas, brushlands, roadsides in the Southwest.

backyard
Queen caterpillars absorb distasteful milkweed toxins and are usually avoided by predators.

ATTRACTING BUTTERFLIES   **243**

EPARGYREUS
CLARUS
SIZE: 1¾–2½″

SILVER-SPOTTED SKIPPER

host plant

Beans, beggar ticks, cassia, false indigo, locust, ticktrefoil.

nectar plant

Bird droppings, aster, ironweed, mistflower, verbena, blue mist shrub, chaste tree.

life cycle

Eggs are green. Caterpillar is yellow-green with vertical lines of dark green speckles. Reddish brown head is large, bulbous, on a tiny neck.

habitat

Canyons, hillsides, meadows, forest clearings, woodlands, barnyards.

backyard

Common in suburban gardens. Look for chewed leaves rolled with silk that hide tiny caterpillars, or larger caterpillars hiding between folded leaves bound with silk.

**PYRGUS
COMMUNIS**
SIZE: 1–2"

COMMON CHECKERED-SKIPPER

host plant
Cheeseweed, globe mallow, hibiscus, hollyhock, poppy mallow, wild mallows.

nectar plant
Aster, beggar ticks, coneflower, fleabane, fogfruit, ironweed, mistflower, blue mist shrub.

life cycle
Eggs are green, fading to pale. Caterpillar is green to pinkish, with many white speckles and short hairs. Head is bulbous, reddish brown.

habitat
Beaches, dry open areas, grasslands, roadsides, weedy places, watercourses.

backyard
One of the most common skippers of cities and developed areas. Small, but males aggressively defend territories.

POLITES
THEMISTOCLES
SIZE: ½–1″

TAWNY-EDGED SKIPPER

host plant

Various grasses, including bluegrass and panic grass.

nectar plant

Alfalfa, bluets, chickory, dogbane, purple coneflower, red clover, thistle.

life cycle

Eggs are green. Caterpillar is reddish or tan, with dark speckles and a dark stripe on back.

habitat

Bogs, eastern grasslands, moist meadows; forest edges and mountains in West.

backyard

Reproduces on common lawn grasses, making this little creature one of the most common skippers in suburban gardens.

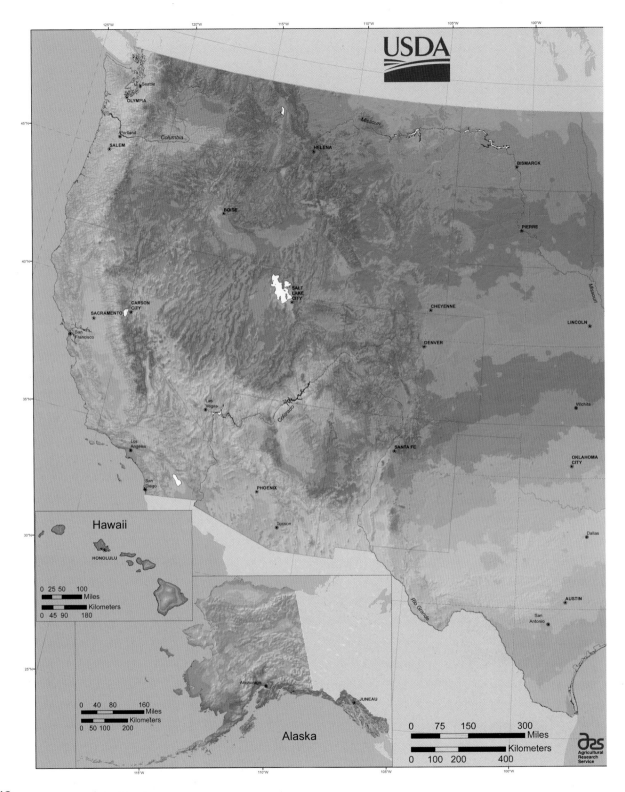

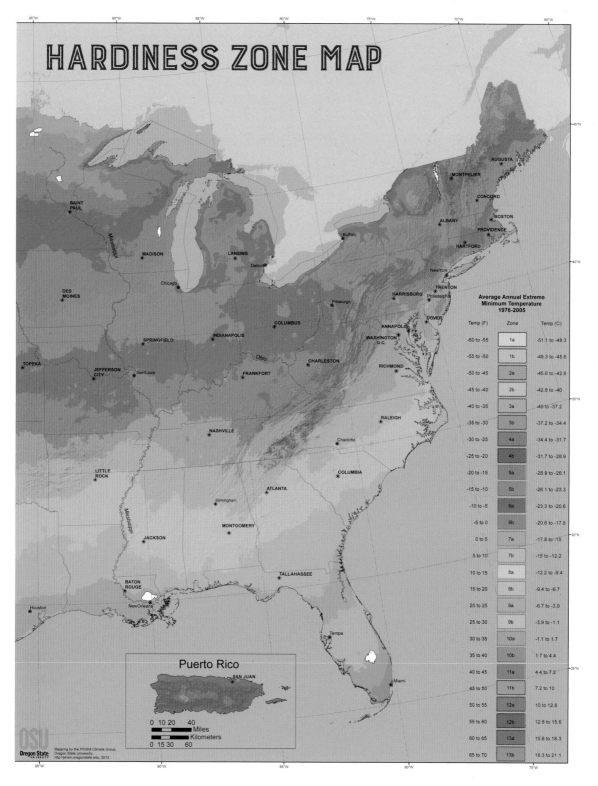

HARDINESS ZONE MAP

Average Annual Extreme Minimum Temperature 1976-2005

Temp (F)	Zone	Temp (C)
-60 to -55	1a	-51.1 to -48.3
-55 to -50	1b	-48.3 to -45.6
-50 to -45	2a	-45.6 to -42.8
-45 to -40	2b	-42.8 to -40
-40 to -35	3a	-40 to -37.2
-35 to -30	3b	-37.2 to -34.4
-30 to -25	4a	-34.4 to -31.7
-25 to -20	4b	-31.7 to -28.9
-20 to -15	5a	-28.9 to -26.1
-15 to -10	5b	-26.1 to -23.3
-10 to -5	6a	-23.3 to -20.6
-5 to 0	6b	-20.6 to -17.8
0 to 5	7a	-17.8 to -15
5 to 10	7b	-15 to -12.2
10 to 15	8a	-12.2 to -9.4
15 to 20	8b	-9.4 to -6.7
20 to 25	9a	-6.7 to -3.9
25 to 30	9b	-3.9 to -1.1
30 to 35	10a	-1.1 to 1.7
35 to 40	10b	1.7 to 4.4
40 to 45	11a	4.4 to 7.2
45 to 50	11b	7.2 to 10
50 to 55	12a	10 to 12.8
55 to 60	12b	12.8 to 15.6
60 to 65	13a	15.6 to 18.3
65 to 70	13b	18.3 to 21.1

Puerto Rico

SAN JUAN

0 10 20 40
Miles
Kilometers
0 15 30 60

OSU
Oregon State
UNIVERSITY

Mapping by the PRISM Climate Group,
Oregon State University,
http://prism.oregonstate.edu, 2012

PHOTO AND ILLUSTRATION CREDITS

Steve Buchanan, 194 (top), 199 (bottom), 200 (top), 201, 203 (bottom), 205 (all)

Janet Davis, ii, iv, vi, 3 (middle), 3 (left), 4, 6 (top), 7 (top), 13, 16, 27, 32, 33, 34, 35, 43, 49, 56, 59, 60, 64, 67, 70, 74, 81, 83 (bottom), 85 (middle), 85 (bottom), 86, 114 (middle), 114 (right), 115 (middle), 116, 124, 129, 131, 133, 134, 142, 152, 153 (top left), 153, (top right), 154 (top right), 154 (bottom right), 156, 159, 164 (left), 164 (right), 165 (top), 166 (right), 167 (right), 168 (right), 169 (top right), 169 (bottom), 186 (right), 187 (right), 191, 194 (bottom), 196, 199 (middle), 202, 203 (top), 203 (middle)

Gilles DeCruyenaere/Shutterstock, 119 (top)

FLPA/Shutterstock, 36

FLPA/Daphne Kinzler/Shutterstock, 155

Siegfried Kuttig/imageBROKER/Shutterstock, 121

Betty Mackey, 3 (right), 7 (bottom), 55

Nancy J. Ondra, i, 2 (left), 2 (middle), 5, 8, 9, 11, 21, 23, 27, 28, 79, 82, 83 (top), 84 (left), 84 (right), 87 (top), 87 (bottom), 115 (right), 119 (bottom), 120 (left), 123, 139, 144, 153 (bottom), 154 (left), 161, 165 (bottom), 167 (left), 168 (left), 169 (top left), 186 (middle), 188, 189, 190, 192, 198, 199 (top), 200 (bottom)

Shutterstock/Agami Photo Agency, 173

Shutterstock/Alan B. Schroeder, 26, 40

Shutterstock/Alexa Zari, 63

Shutterstock/alslutsky, 215

Shutterstock/Angel Dibilio, 180

Shutterstock/Aniana, 149

Shutterstock/Anthony Heflin, 225

Shutterstock/Arto Hakola, 212

Shutterstock/Az Outdoor Photography, 171

Shutterstock/Birdiegal, 90

Shutterstock/Bonnie Taylor Barry, 93 (left), 111

Shutterstock/Boris Novikov, 213

Shutterstock/Brian Lasenby, 95, 109, 112

Shutterstock/Chris Hill, 107

Shutterstock/Damann, 50

Shutterstock/Danita Delmont, 141, 239

Shutterstock/David Byron Keener, 228

Shutterstock/David Havel, 172

Shutterstock/Dec Hogan, 178

Shutterstock/Dennis W. Donohue, 182

Shutterstock/Elizabeth Spencer, 238

Shutterstock/Evelyn D. Harrison, 177

Shutterstock/Fotorequest, 89 (right), 92

Shutterstock/Frode Jacobsen, 218, 221, 234, 240, 241

Shutterstock/Ger Bosma Photos, 236

Shutterstock/Gerald A. Deboer, 245

Shutterstock/I. Rottlaender, 114 (left), 162

Shutterstock/Islavicek, 27, 45

Shutterstock/Iva Vagnerova, 26, 46

Shutterstock/James W. Thompson, 207

Shutterstock/Jayne Gulbrand 105 (right)

Shutterstock/Jeff Holcombe, 235

Shutterstock/Jim And Lynne Weber, 219

Shutterstock/Kajonsak Tui, 226

Shutterstock/Keneva Photography, 176

Shutterstock/Laura Mountainspring, 110

Shutterstock/Leena Robinson, 243

Shutterstock/Lorraine Hudgins, 103

Shutterstock/Marco Uliana, 222

Shutterstock/Marek R. Swadzba, 233

Shutterstock/Matt Cuda, 89 (left)

Shutterstock/Maximsuntar 104 (right)

Shutterstock/Mel Toppi, 227

Shutterstock/Melinda Fawver, 237

Shutterstock/Nico Giuliani, 181

Shutterstock/Paul Reeves Photography, 99, 108 (left), 186 (left), 216, 232

Shutterstock/Peter Turner Photography, 39

Shutterstock/Phil Lowe, 94

Shutterstock/Photosounds, 115 (left), 150

Shutterstock/Ramona Edwards, 174

Shutterstock/Randy Bjorklund, 183, 214, 223

Shutterstock/Richard G. Smith, 224

Shutterstock/Robert L. Kothenbeutel, 104 (left), 108 (right)

Shutterstock/Sari Oneal, 187 (middle), 208, 211, 217

Shutterstock/senengmotret, 246

Shutterstock/Serguei Koultchitskii, 210

Shutterstock/Sharon Haeger, 229

Shutterstock/Shawn Hempe, 220

Shutterstock/Steve Byland, 96, 97, 101, 102, 184

Shutterstock/Steven Fowler, 244

Shutterstock/Steven R. Smith, 230, 231, 242

Shutterstock/sumikophoto, 175

Shutterstock/Takahashi Photography, 185

Shutterstock/Tamu1500, 26, 73

Shutterstock/Tim Zurowski, 91, 98, 100, 105 (left), 106, 113

Shutterstock/Tom Reichner, 93 (right), 179

Shutterstock/yhelfman, 209

Lisa A. White, 187 (left), 195

Doreen Wynja, 6 (bottom), 120 (right)

Doreen Wynja at Petals & Butterflies Farm Nursery BC, 15

Doreen Wynja in Steve and Ann Zazzi Seattle garden, 19

Julie Zickefoose, 2 (right), 14, 17, 25, 29, 30, 31, 53, 85 (top), 117, 147, 166 (left), 193, 197, 247

COVER:

Background photo © Kesu01 / Depositphotos

Photos on left, from top to bottom: © Janet Davis, © Nancy J. Ondra, © Janet Davis, © Nancy J. Ondra

INDEX

Buckeyes, 203, 204, 240
Buckthorns, 66, 205
Buckwheats, 202, 223, 227, 237
Buddleia, 152, 204
Buffaloberries, 66
Buffalo grass, 86
Buff-bellied hummingbird, 183
Bullock's oriole, 108
Buntings, 72, 80
Burdock, 191, 235
Bur oak, 65
Butterflies. *See also names of specific butterflies*
  cover and nest sites for, 16–23
  flowers for, 25, 82, 84, 85, 192, 194–203
  food for, 5–12
  sunning spots for, 193
  trees, shrubs, and vines for, 204–5
  water for, 193
Butterfly bushes
  in butterfly gardens, 204
  for hummingbirds, 152
  as nectar plants for butterflies, 207–9, 211, 213, 228, 236, 239, 242
Butterfly milkweed, 219, 224, 243
Butterfly weed, 84, 85, 198, 199

C

Cabbage, 190, 203, 214
Cabbage white butterfly, 203
Caesalpinia gilliesii, 167
Calendula officinalis, 82
California black oak, 65
California buckeye, 240
California fuchsia, 168
California grape, 80
California poppy, 82, 83
Calliope hummingbird, 117, 181
Callistemon, 167
  citrinus, 166, 167
  eriophylla, 167
  rigidus, 167
Callistephus chinensis, 82
Callophrys augustinus, 223
Calothorax lucifer, 173

Calypte
  anna, 176 (*See also* Anna's hummingbird)
  costae, 177 (*See also* Costa's hummingbird)
Camassia, 202
Campanula, 202
Campion, 152
Campsis, 156–57. *See also* trumpet vine
  radicans, 35, 119, 156–57; 'Crimson Trumpet', 157
  × *tagliabuana* 'Mme. Galen', 157
Canada jay, 91
Canada lily, 135
Canada violet, 201
Canada wild rye, 86
Canna × *generalis*, 127
Cannas, 127
Canyon grape, 80
Canyon live oak, 65
Cape honeysuckle, 168
Caragana arborescens, 164
Cardinal climber, 158
Cardinal flower, 136, 202, 212, 220
Cardinalis cardinalis, 111
Cardinals
  flowers for, 80
  food for, 9, 30
  northern, 111
  shrubs and brambles, 68, 72, 75, 78
  trees for, 41, 44, 47, 48, 57, 62, 65
  vines for, 80
Carex, 191
Carmine crab apple, 55
Carnations, 152
Carolina chickadee, 93
Carolina phlox, 145
Carolina rose, 72
Carolina wren, 31, 96
Carpinus caroliniana, 204
Carrot, 200, 208, 209
Carya, 37
Caryopteris, 204
Cassia, 197, 244
Castilleja, 152

Catbirds
  food for, 9, 10, 36
  gray, 101
  shrubs and brambles, 68, 69, 71, 75, 76, 78
  trees for, 42, 47, 51, 52, 54, 62
Catbriers, 80
Catchfly, 152
Catmint, 6, 198
Catnip, 198
Cauliflower, 203
Ceanothus, 204
  americanus, 204
  cordulatus, 204
  fendleri, 204
  integerrimus, 204
  thyrsiflorus, 204
Cedars, 17, 37. *See also* eastern red cedar; western red cedar
Cedar waxwing, 42, 103
Celastrina ladon, 226. *See also* spring azure butterfly
Celastris
  orbiculatus, 80
  scandens, 80
Celtis, 44–45, 204. *See also* hackberries
  laevigata, 44
  occidentalis, 44–45
Centaurea, 195
  cyanus, 82, 196
Centranthus ruber, 202
Century plant, 167
Cercidium floridum, 167
Cercis, 197
Cercyonis pegala, 241
Cestrum, 167
  aurantiacum, 167
  elegans, 167
  fasciculatum, 167
Chaenomeles speciosa, 164
Chamaecyparis, 37
Chasmanthium latifolium, 20, 86, 87
Chaste tree, 164, 165, 205, 235, 244
Checkered-skipper, common, 245
Checkered white butterfly, 214
Cheeseweed, 245

pipevine, 189, 207
spicebush, 212
water for, 193
western tiger, 189, 204
zebra, 189, 213
Swamp milkweed, 84, 198, 207
Sweet alyssum, 203, 221
Sweet bay, 204, 211
Sweet cherries, 62
Sweet clovers, 197
Sweet pea, 196–97
Sweet pepperbush, 204
Sweet scabious, 202
Sweet violet, 201
Sweet William, 82, 118, 145, 154, 202
Switch grass, 86
Sycamores, 37, 189, 204
Symphoricarpus, 66
　albus, 66
　occidentalis, 66
　orbiculatus, 66
Syringa, 164, 205
　vulgaris, 165

T

Tagetes, 82, 154, 196. *See also* marigold
Tanagers, 32, 42, 62, 75, 77
　scarlet, 57, 109
　western, 110
Taraxacum officinale, 196
Tart cherries, 62
Tatarian dogwood, 68
Tawny daylily, 131
Tawny-edged skipper, 246
Taxus, 66
Tayberries, 75
Tea crab apple, 55
Tecomaria capensis, 168
Texas mulberry, 57
Texas sage, 146
Thalictrum, 202
Thistle butterfly. *See* painted lady butterfly
Thistles
　in butterfly gardens, 191, 196

globe, 84
　as host plants for butterflies, 235
　as nectar plants for butterflies, 207–8, 211, 212, 217, 219–20, 229–31, 236, 239, 246
Thrashers, 44, 76, 77, 78, 80
Thrushes
　food for, 9, 14
　shrubs and brambles, 68, 72, 77, 78
　trees for, 42, 44, 47, 52, 62
　wood, 99
Thryothorus ludovicianus, 96. *See also* Carolina wren
Thuja occidentalis, 37
Thyme, 198
Thymus, 198
Tickseed, 84, 195
Tickseed sunflower, 221, 235
Tick trefoil, 225, 244
Tiger lily, 135
Tithonia rotundifolia, 82, 154, 196. *See also* Mexican sunflower
Titmice, 44, 61, 77
　tufted, 33, 94
Toadflax, 237
Towhees
　eastern, 105
　flowers for, 80
　food for, 20, 30
　shrubs and brambles, 71, 72, 77, 78
　spotted, 105
　trees for, 38, 42, 44, 61
Tree swallows, 33, 35
Tree tobacco, 168, 169
Trefoil, 216
Trifolium, 197. *See also* clovers
　pratense, 197
Tropaeolum
　majus, 148
　speciosum, 168
True mints, 198
Trumpet flower, 168
Trumpet honeysuckle, 160–61

Trumpet vine, 35, 119, 156–57
Tsuga, 37
　canadensis, 37
　caroliniana, 37
Tufted hairgrass, 86
Tufted titmouse, 33, 94
Tulip tree, 37, 204, 211
Turdus migratorius, 100. *See also* American robin
Turkeys, wild, 61, 71
Turk's-cap lily, 135

U

Urtica, 191

V

Vaccinium, 20, 77, 205. *See also* blueberries
　angustifolium, 77
　ashei, 77
　corymbosum, 77
　pallidum, 77
　stamineum, 77
　vitis idaea, 77
Valley oak, 65
Vanessa
　atalanta, 236 (*See also* red admiral butterfly)
　cardui, 235 (*See also* painted lady butterfly)
Variegated fritillary, 7, 191
Verbena, 150–51, 219, 224, 228, 230, 235, 243–44. *See also* shrub verbena
　'Flame', 151
　× *hybrida*, 150–51
　peruviana, 151
　'Taylortown Red', 151
Vermillion nasturtium, 168
Vernonia, 195–96
　noveboracensis, 84 (*See also* ironweed)
Vervain, 237
Vetches, 197, 216, 217, 225